Beautiful Circles

Mini

Coloring Book

Hand Drawn by Artist

Dwyanna Stoltzfus

Join the Fun!!

Share your colored pages!!

You are invited to color the pages

From this and future publications by

Dwyanna Stoltzfus. Then scan and post

Your colored creations in

Oodles of Doodles

Adult Coloring Group

On facebook

https://www.facebook.com/groups/1519357628356169/

Join Oodles of Doodles Adult Coloring Group,

And have fun sharing your colored pages

And meeting new coloring friends.

Members of the group will also have access

To free coloring pages.

You are welcome to share your colored pages on

Any social network, make sure to mention the title of

The book and the author/artist name.

Uncolored images may not be shared.

You are invited to view Dwyanna's art on

Society 6 at

https://society6.com/dwyanna

And on Red Bubble at

http://www.redbubble.com/people/ilovedoodleart/portfolio

PDF Printable coloring pages available

On Etsy at

https://www.etsy.com/your/shops/DesignsbyDwyanna/onboarding/listings

Follow Dwyanna's art on facebook at

Oodles of Doodles with

Dwyanna Stoltzfus

https://www.facebook.com/pages/Oodles-of-Doodles-with-Dwyanna-Stoltzfus/743502922387046

About:

Get ready to color 50 beautiful small circles full of intricate doodle art designs by Artist Dwyanna Stoltzfus. This adult coloring book is small, only 6 X 9 inches and can easily fit into your bag and go where ever you go. It's a great one to take along when you know you will be waiting somewhere. This coloring book will provide many hours of fun, entertainment. It will also provide hours of peaceful calm and relaxation.

Coloring is not just for children. We encourage our precious children to draw and color as a relaxing quiet activity. Coloring can have the same relaxing/calming effect on adults. It is especially beneficial to those who struggle with anxiety or stress. It's the perfect stress relief.

In this adult coloring book you will find 50 amazing illustrations, printed one per page. A collection of 50 stunning images inspired by doodle art. You will find beautiful intricate flowers, swirls, and many detailed doodle patterns.

You can use this coloring book to help you relax and unwind or just to have fun. You can color the illustrations simply or add depth by shading. Crayons is not recommended for the intricate detail. You can color with fine tip markers, gel pens, and colored pencils.

Enjoy the experience of coloring!!

But most of all relax and have fun!!

Coloring tips:

If you desire to add depth to your coloring you can shade with colored pencils. Use dark colors around edges and into the peaks. Blend in light colors for the middle and more open spaces. You can use black to darken areas, and white to lighten and brighten areas.

Acknowledgments

Thank You to my family for all your support

of my art and this project.

I could not have done it without you!!

Thank You God for the gift and love

Of art and drawing!!

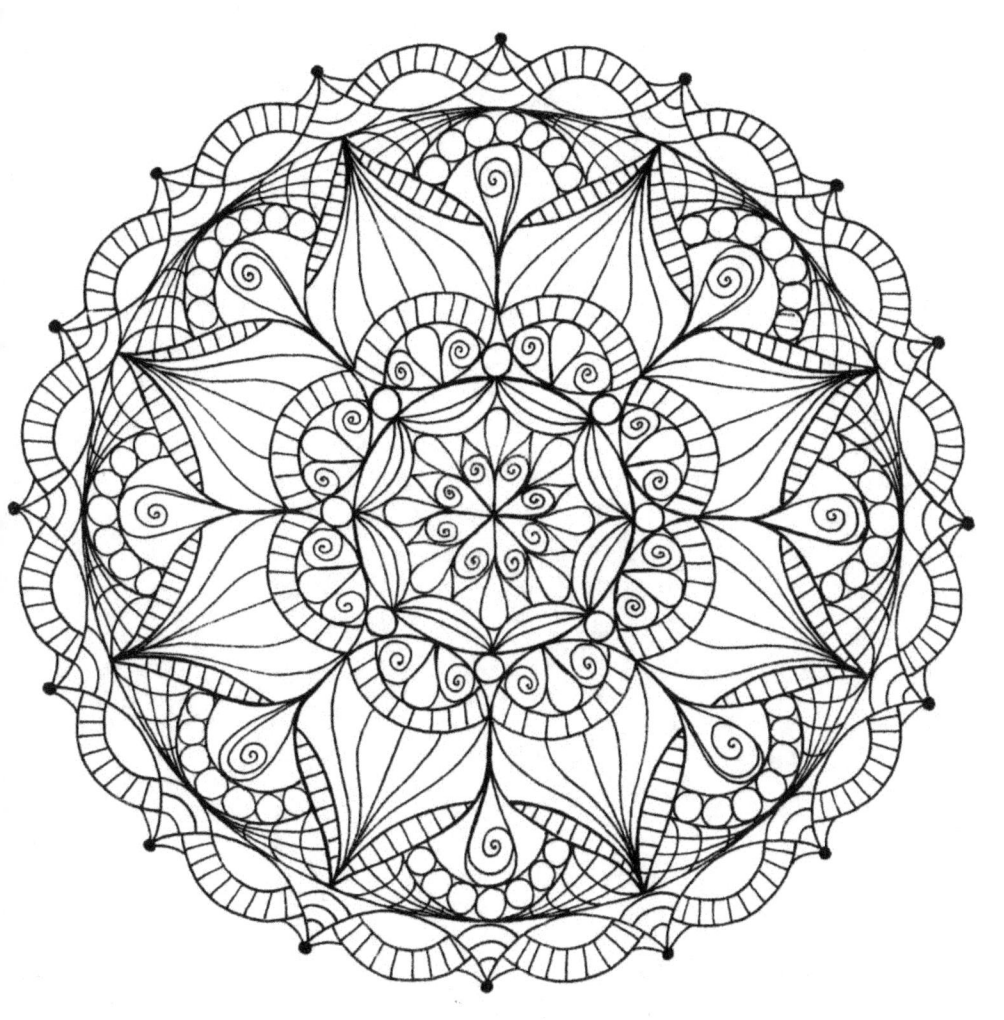

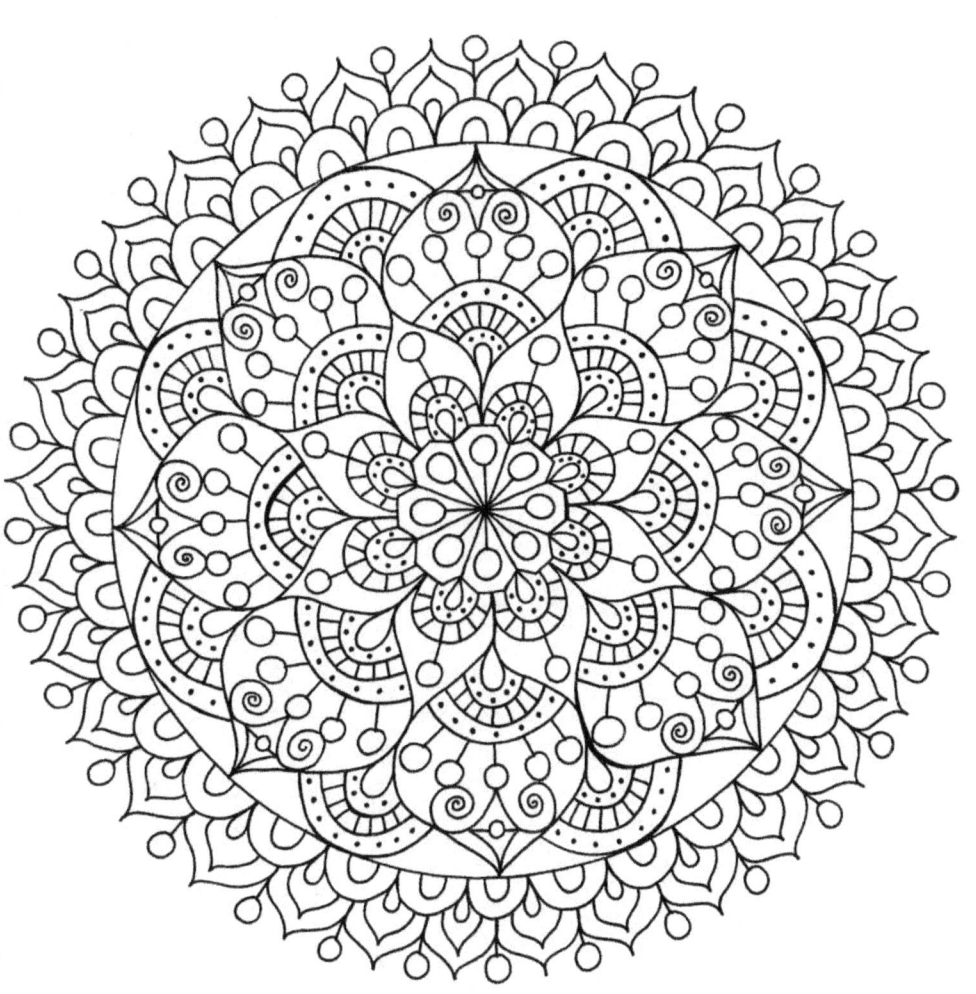

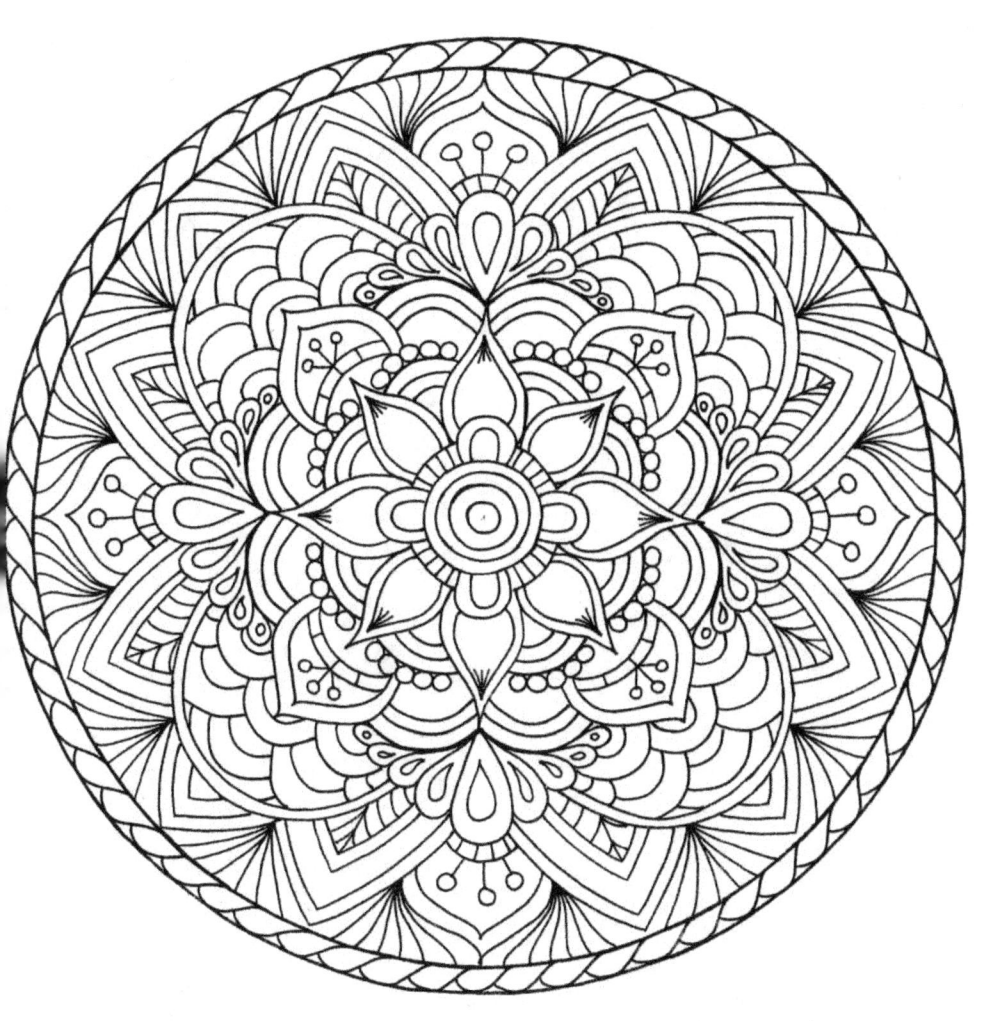

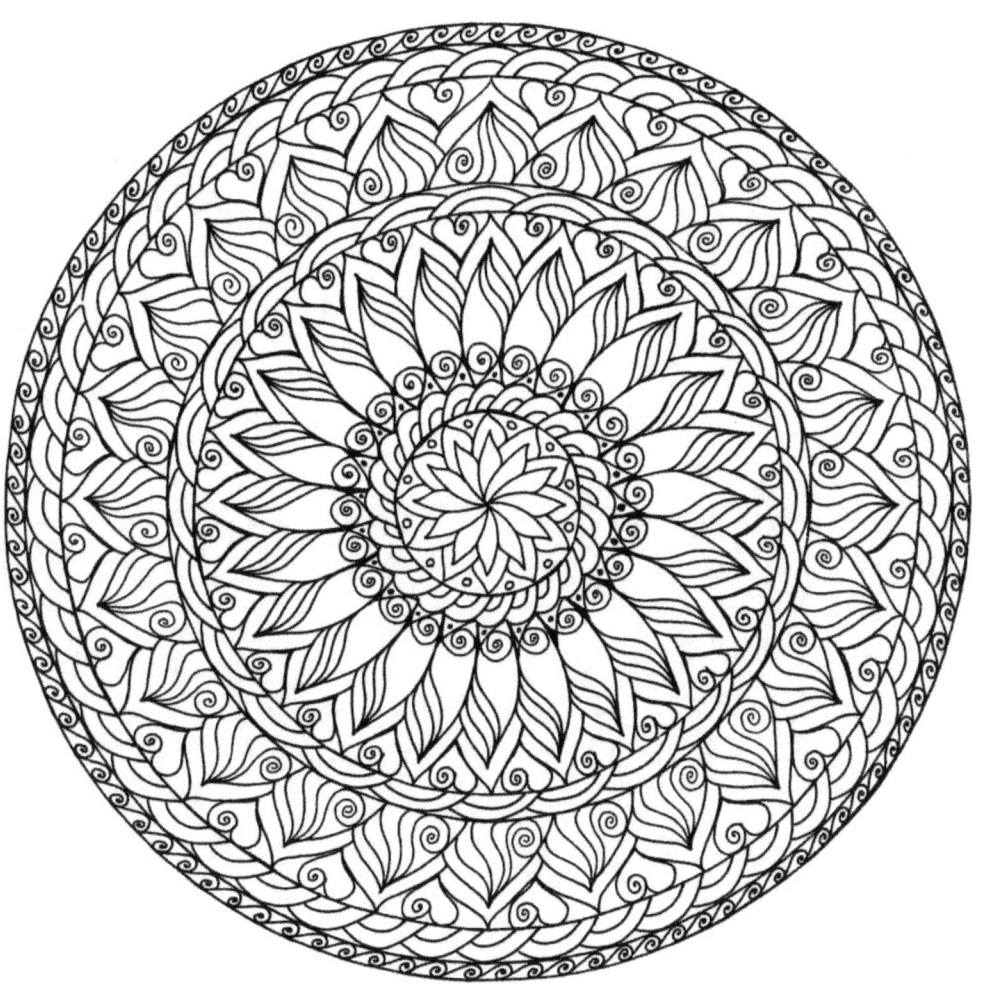

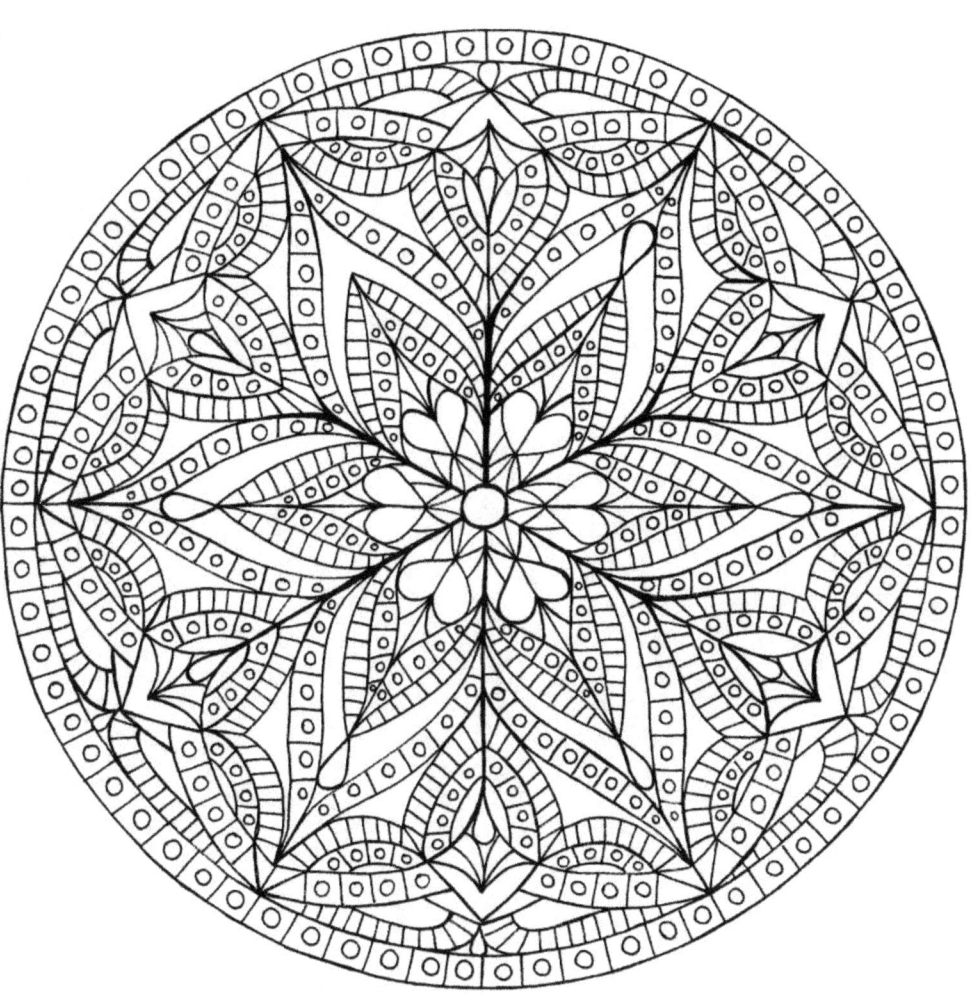

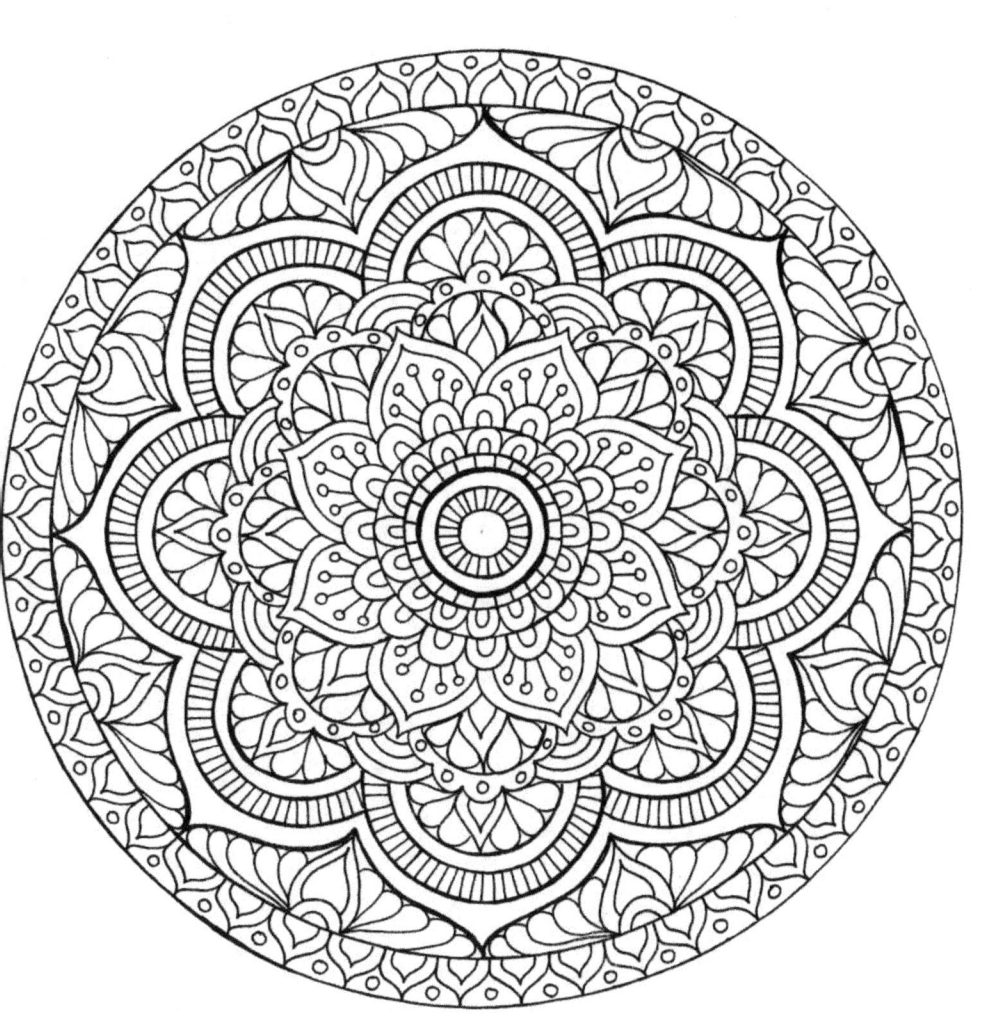

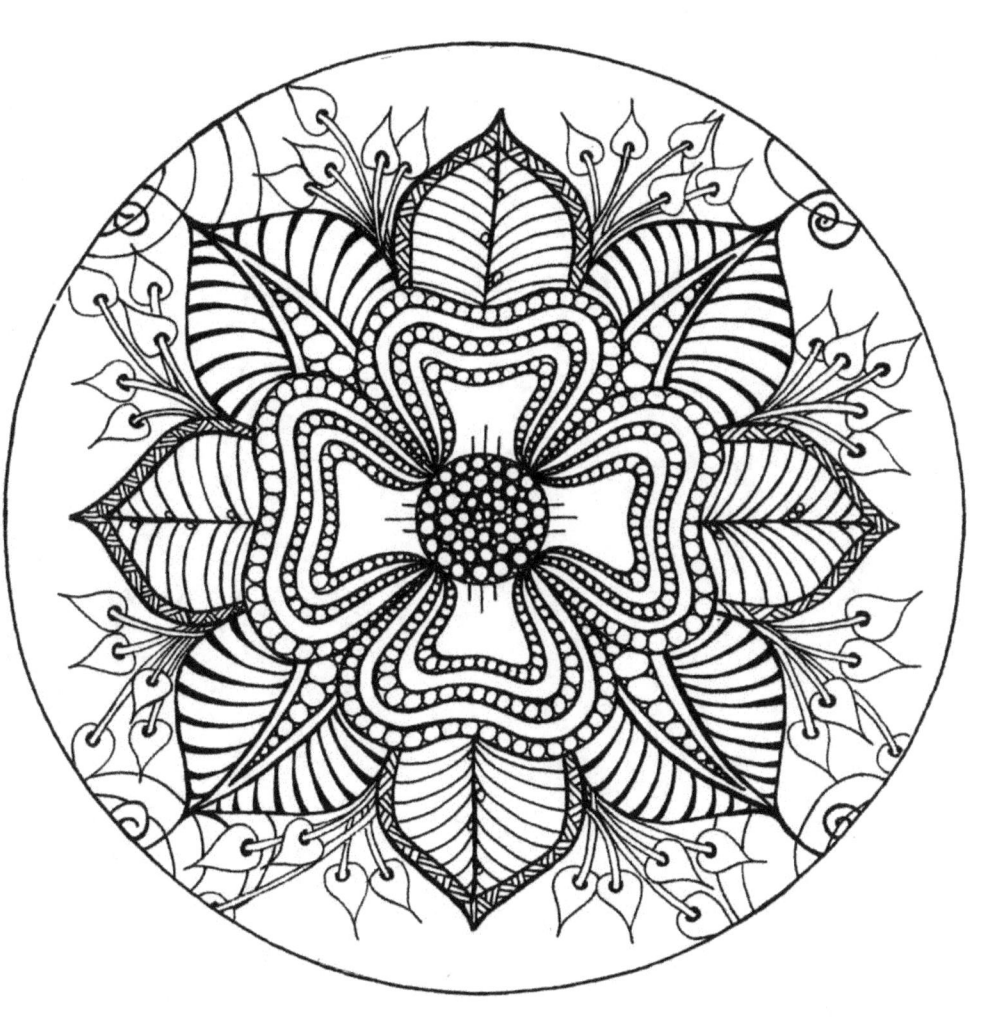

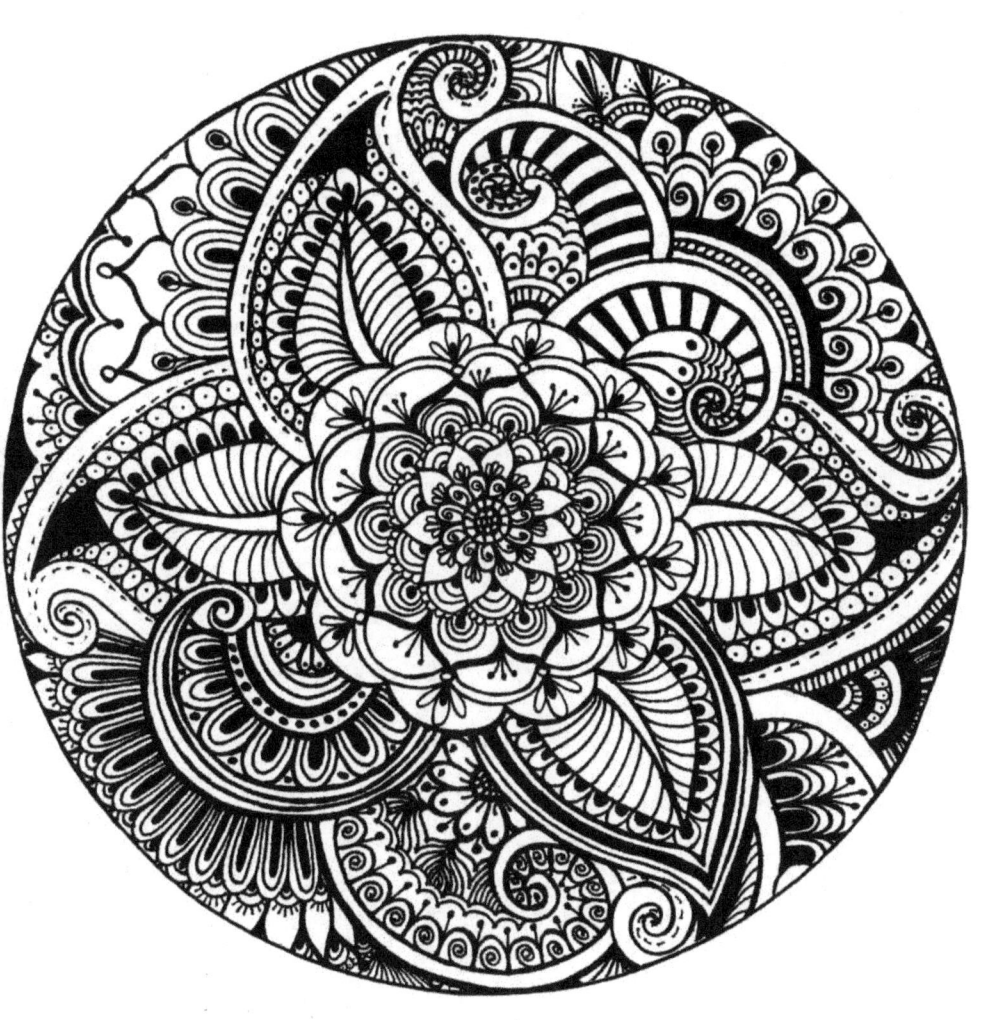

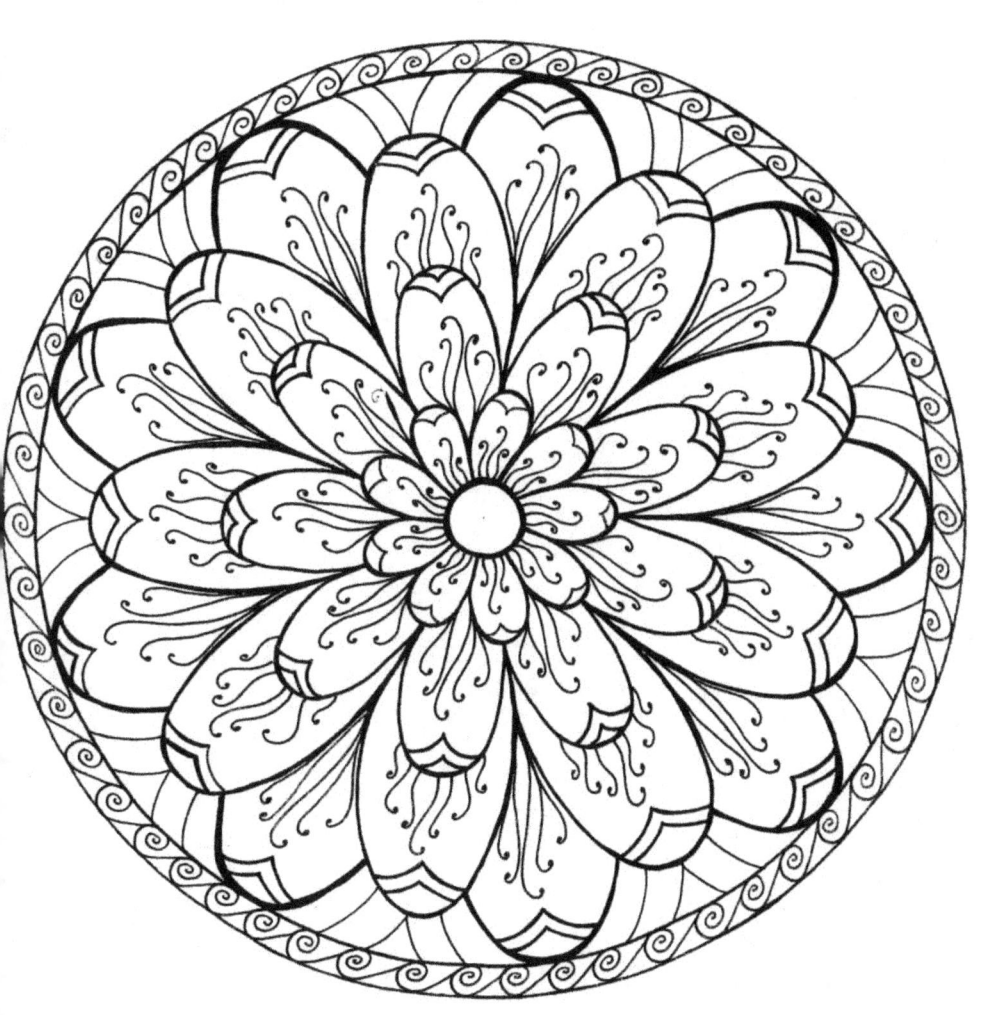

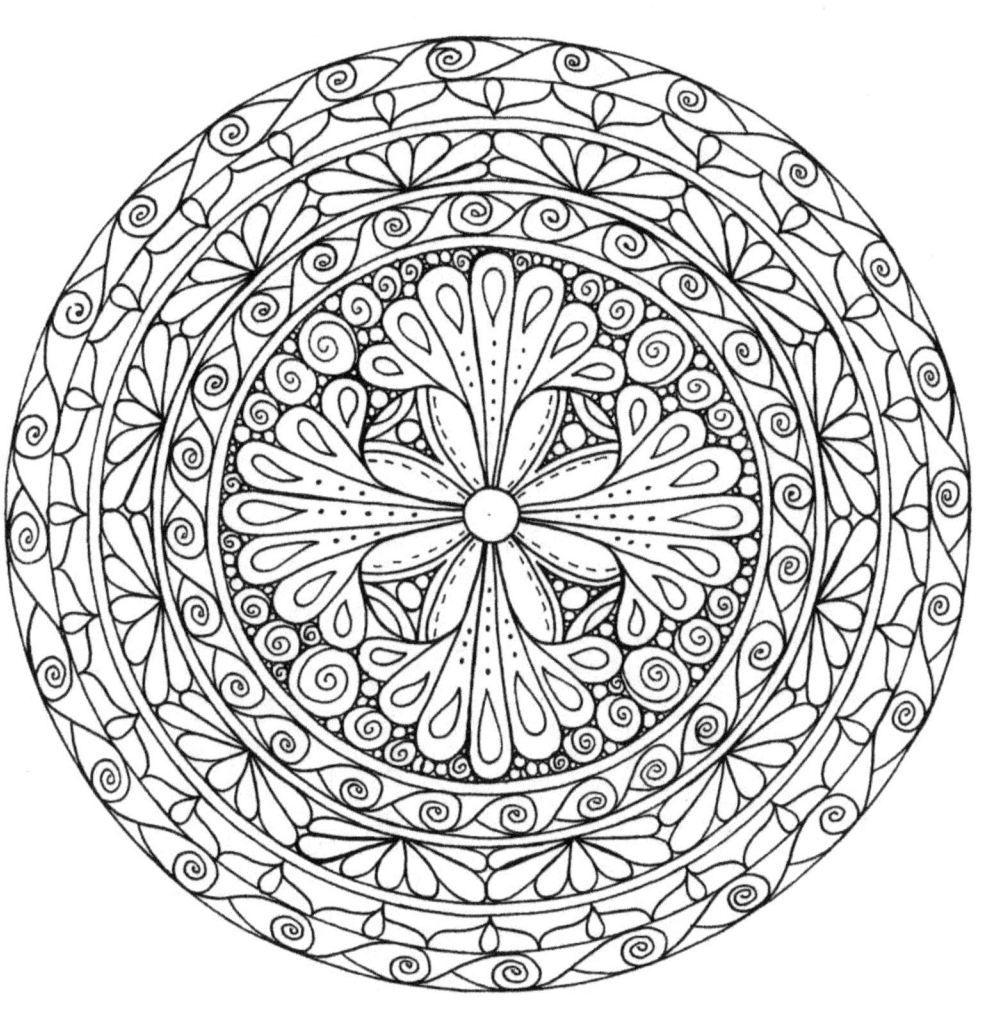

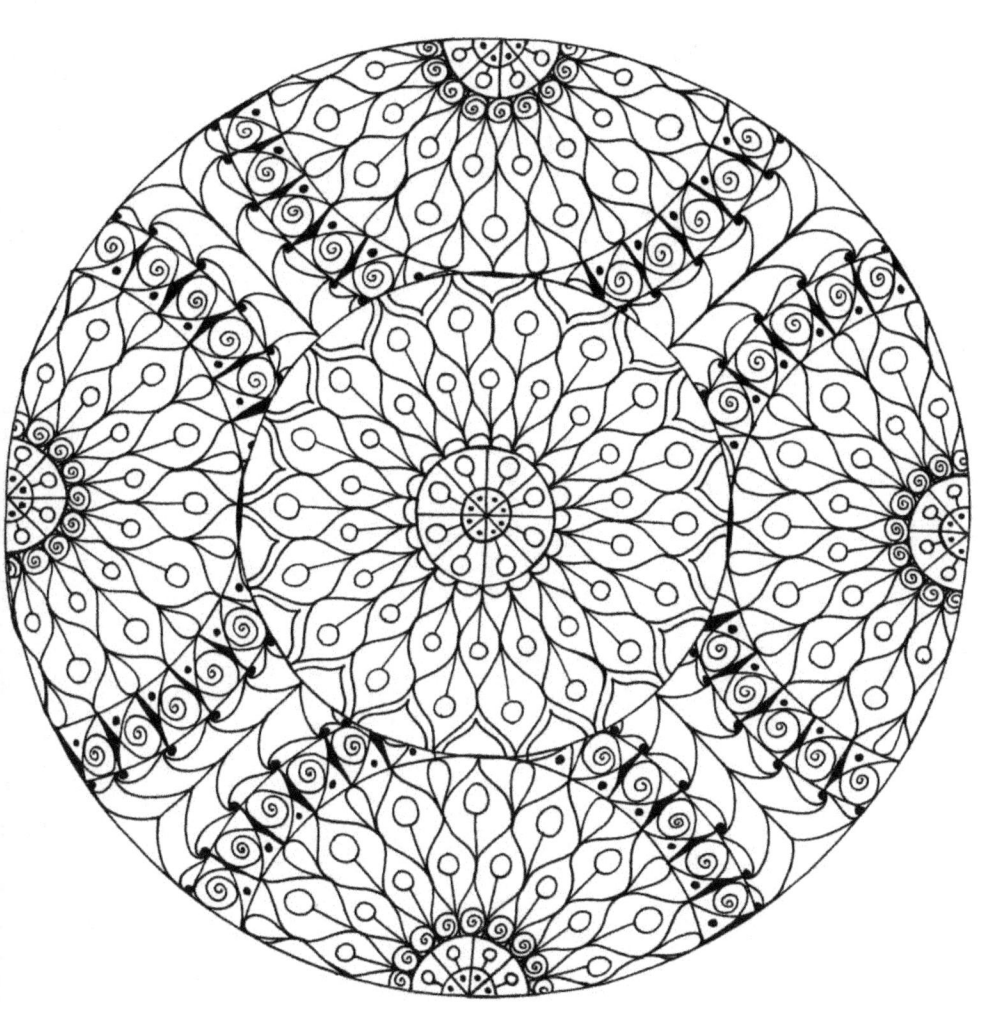

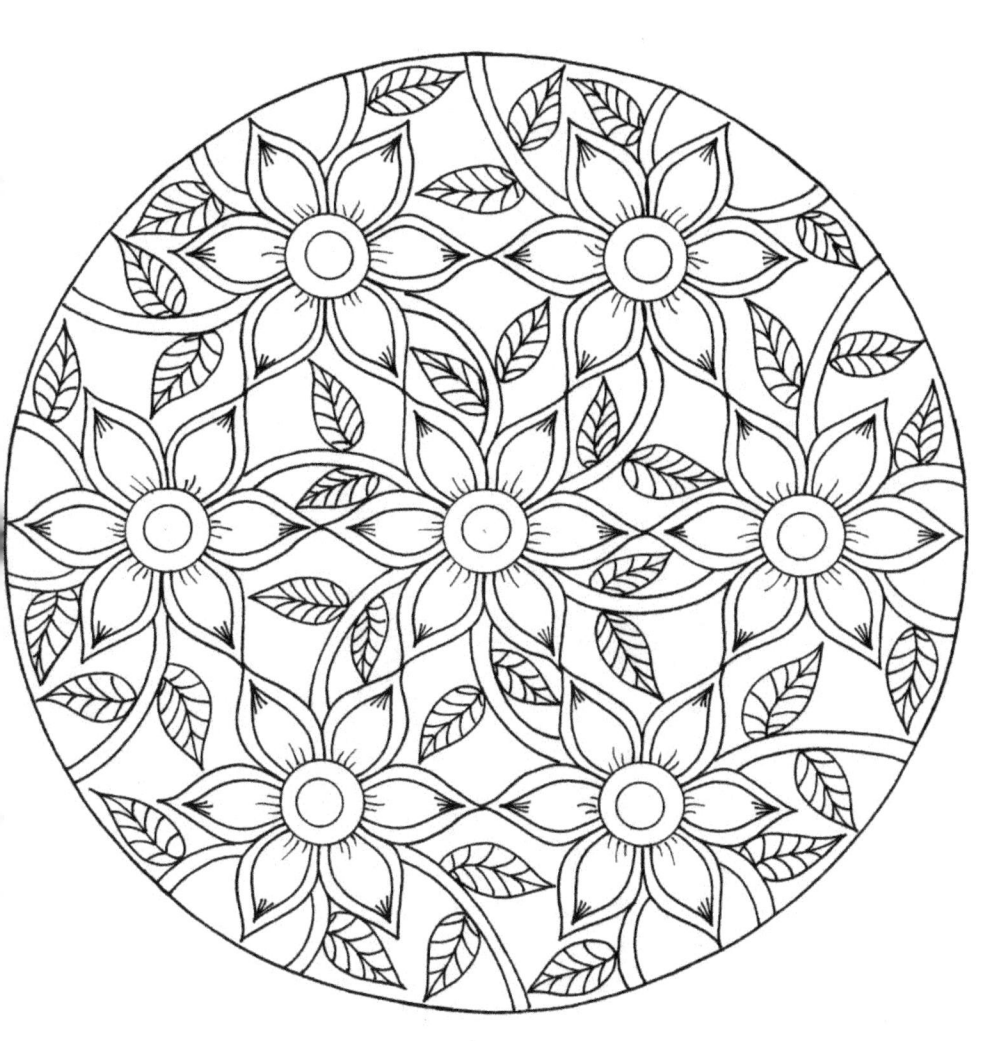

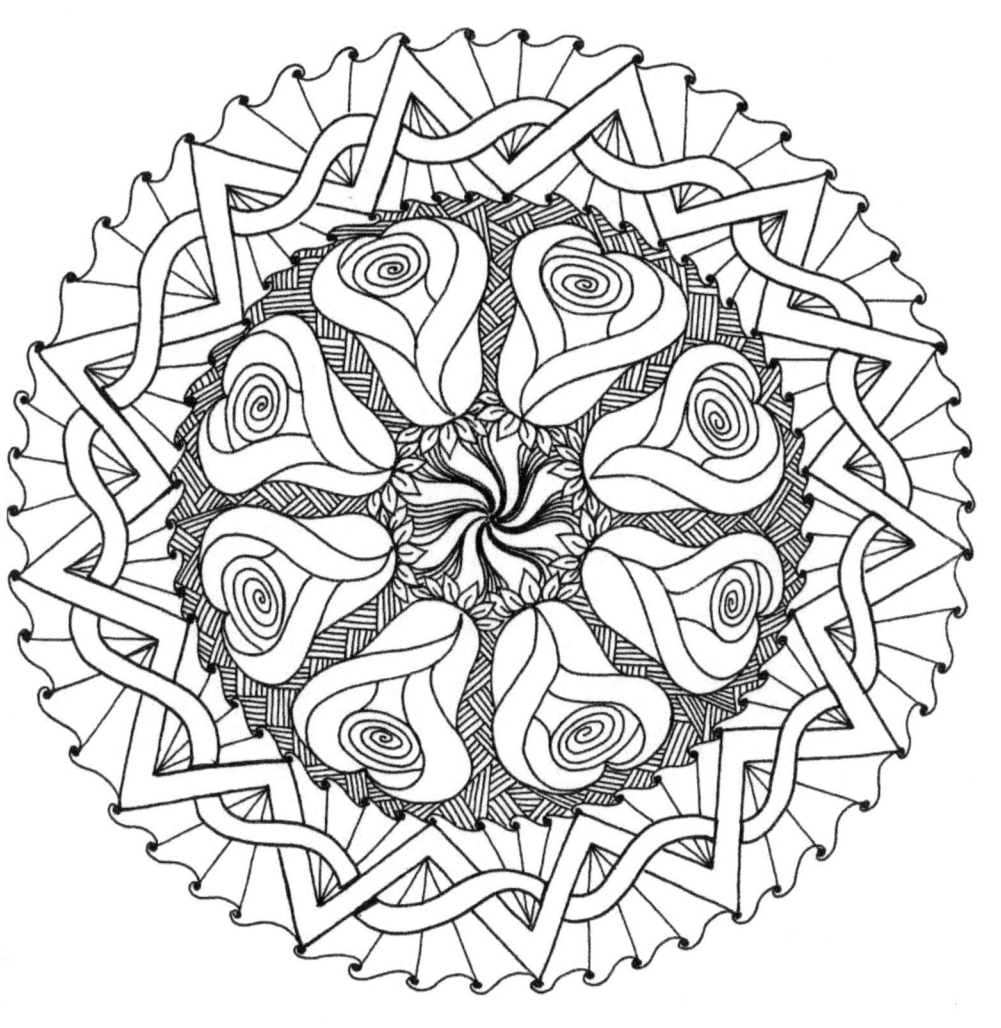

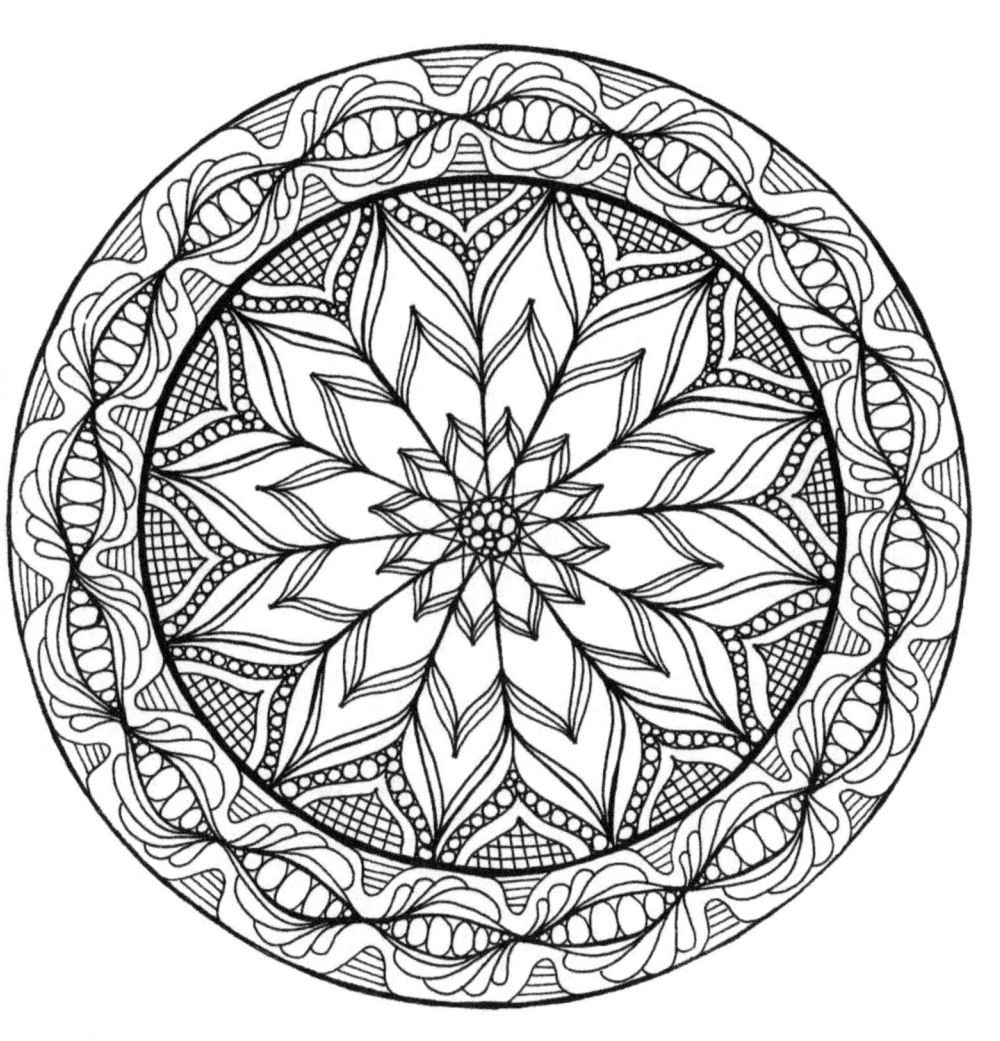

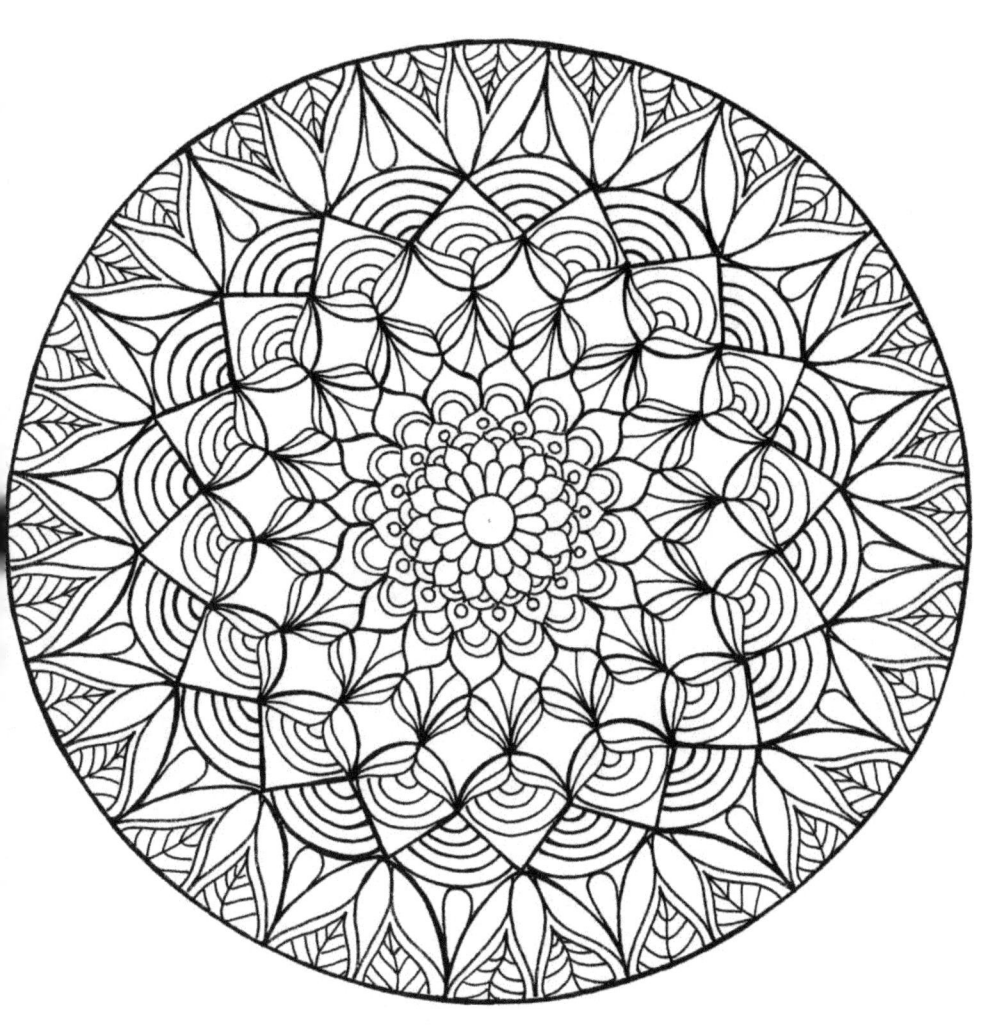

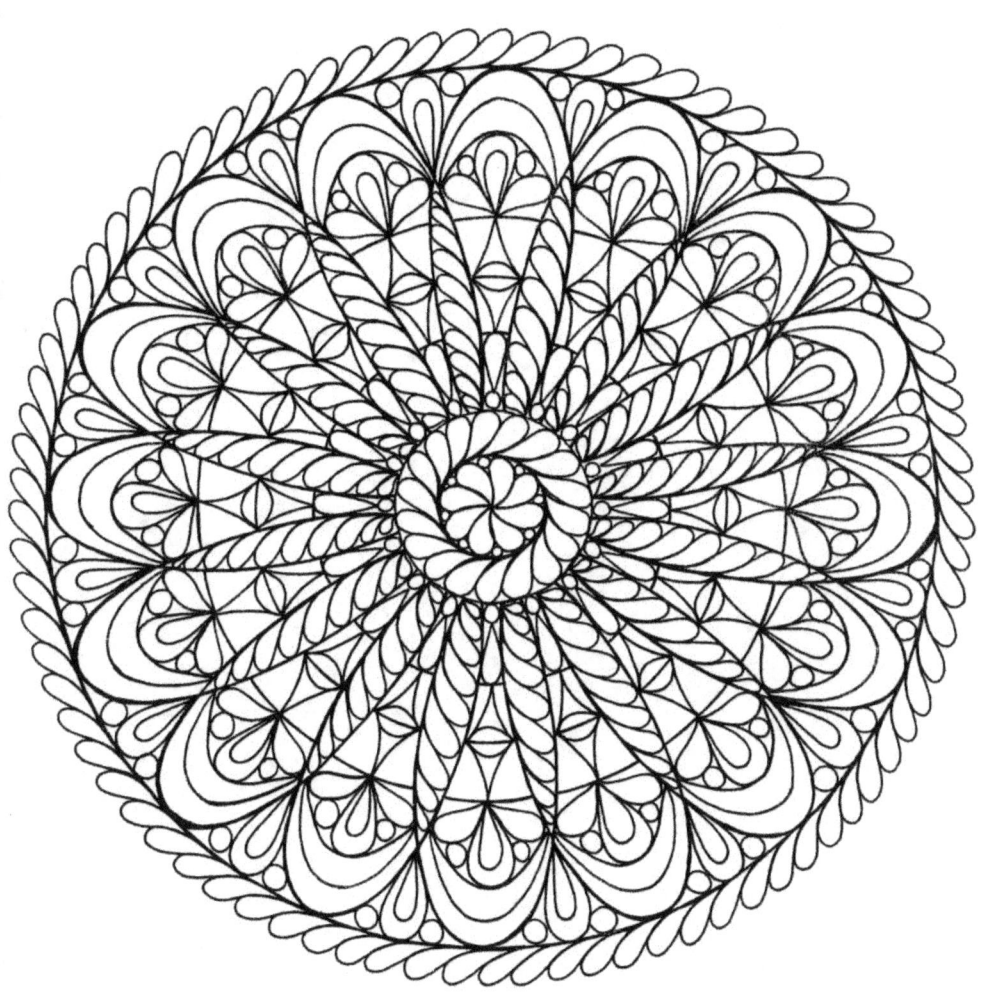

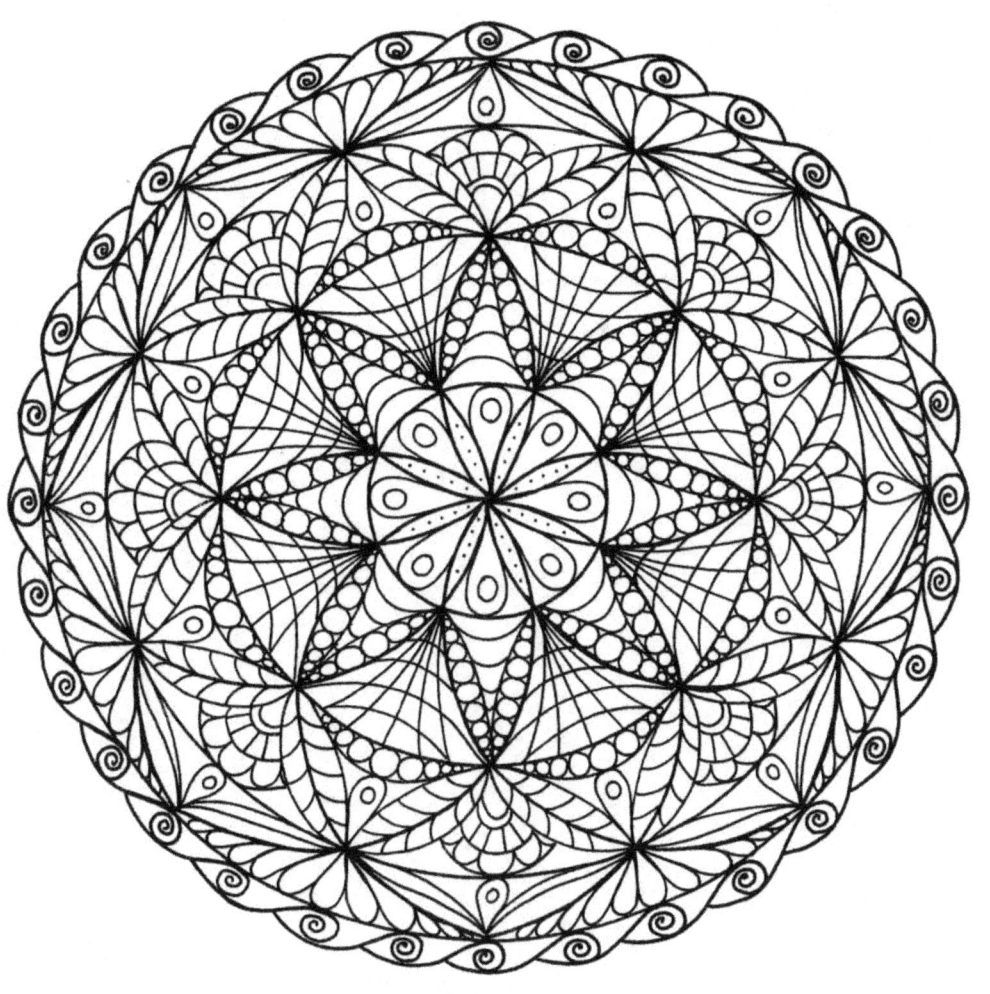

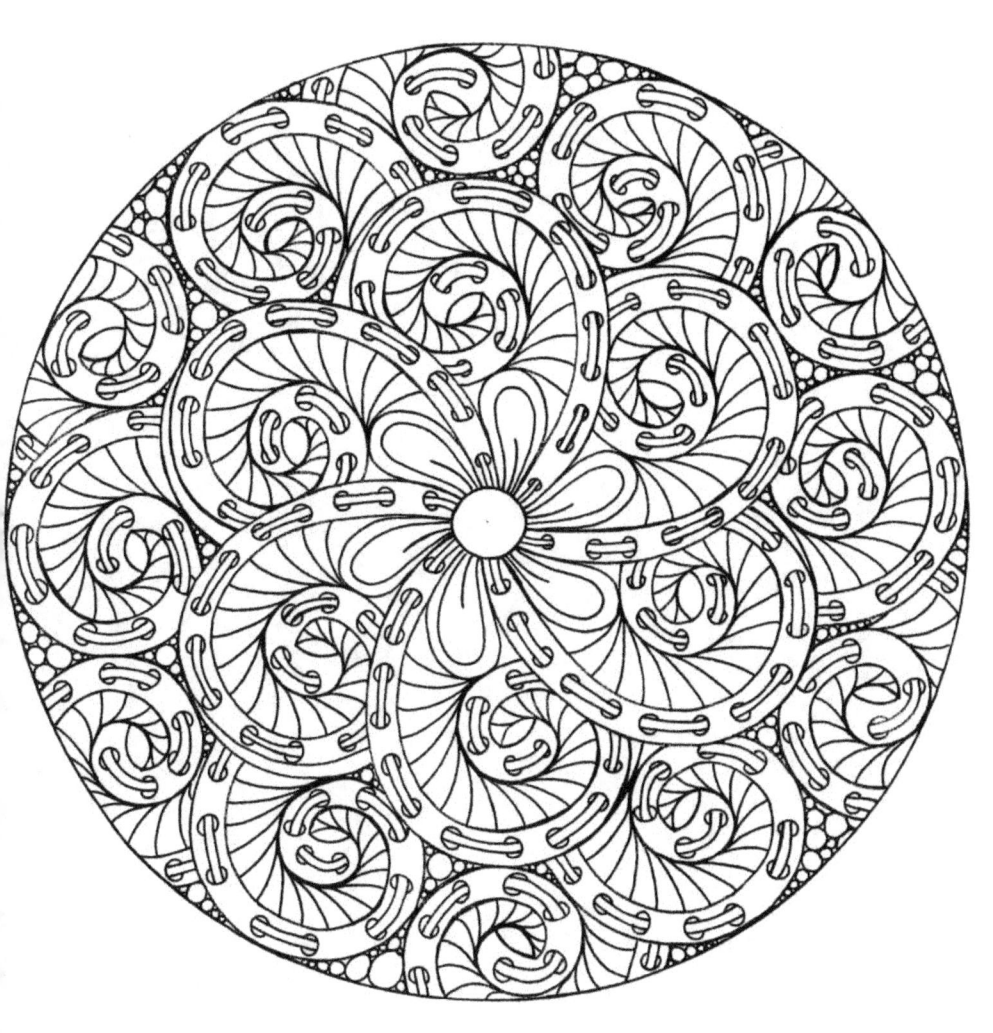

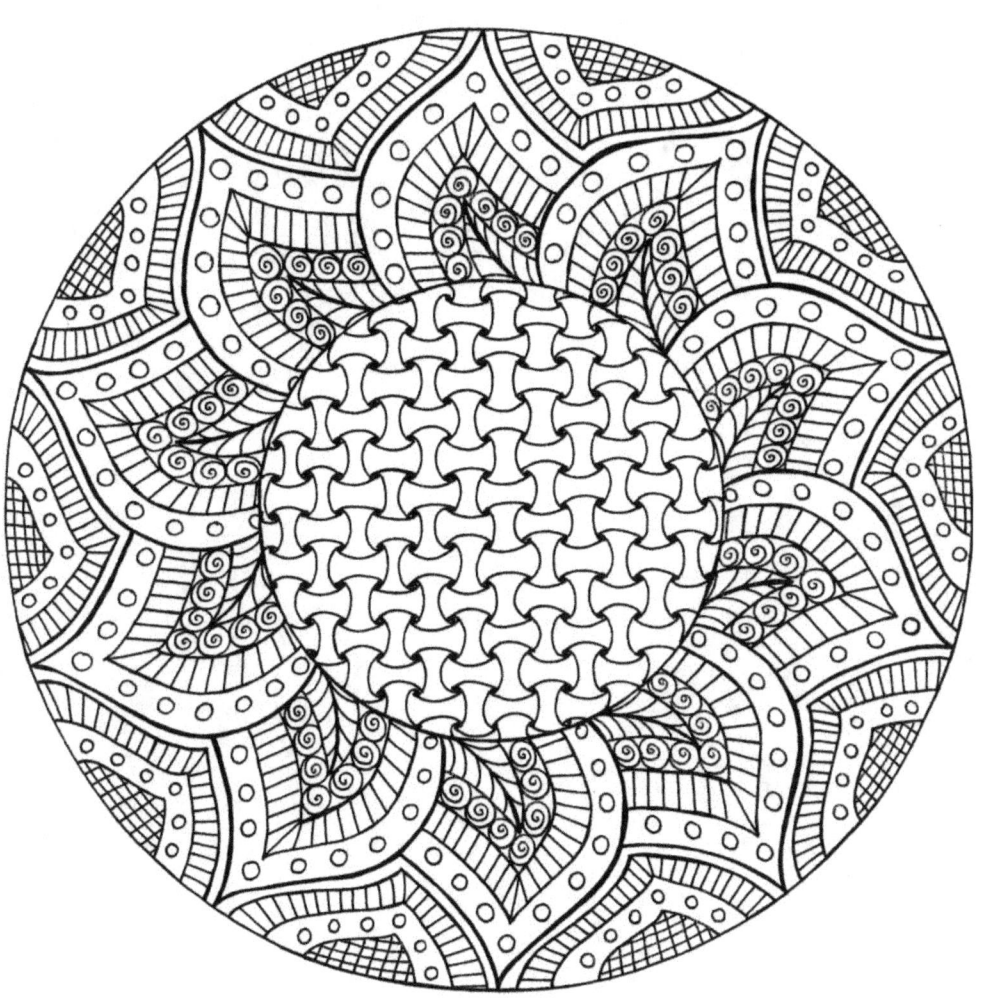

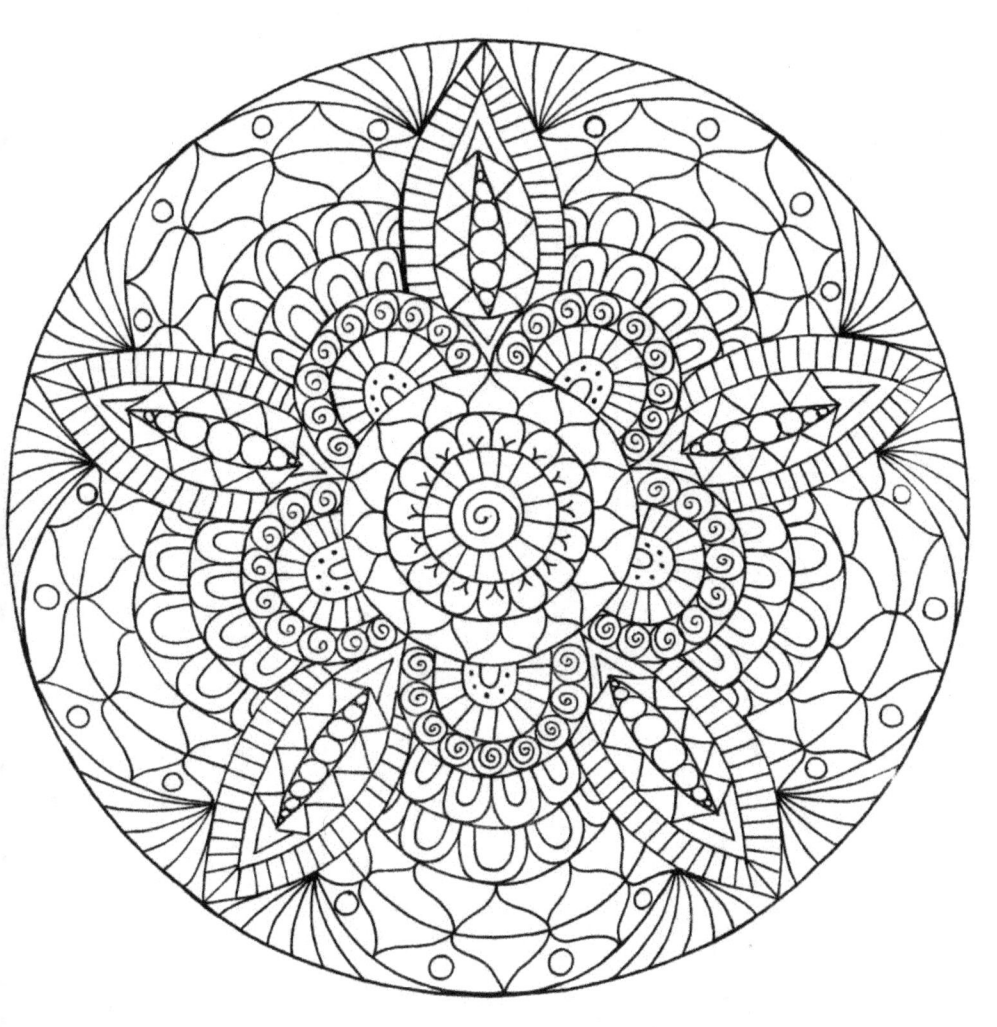

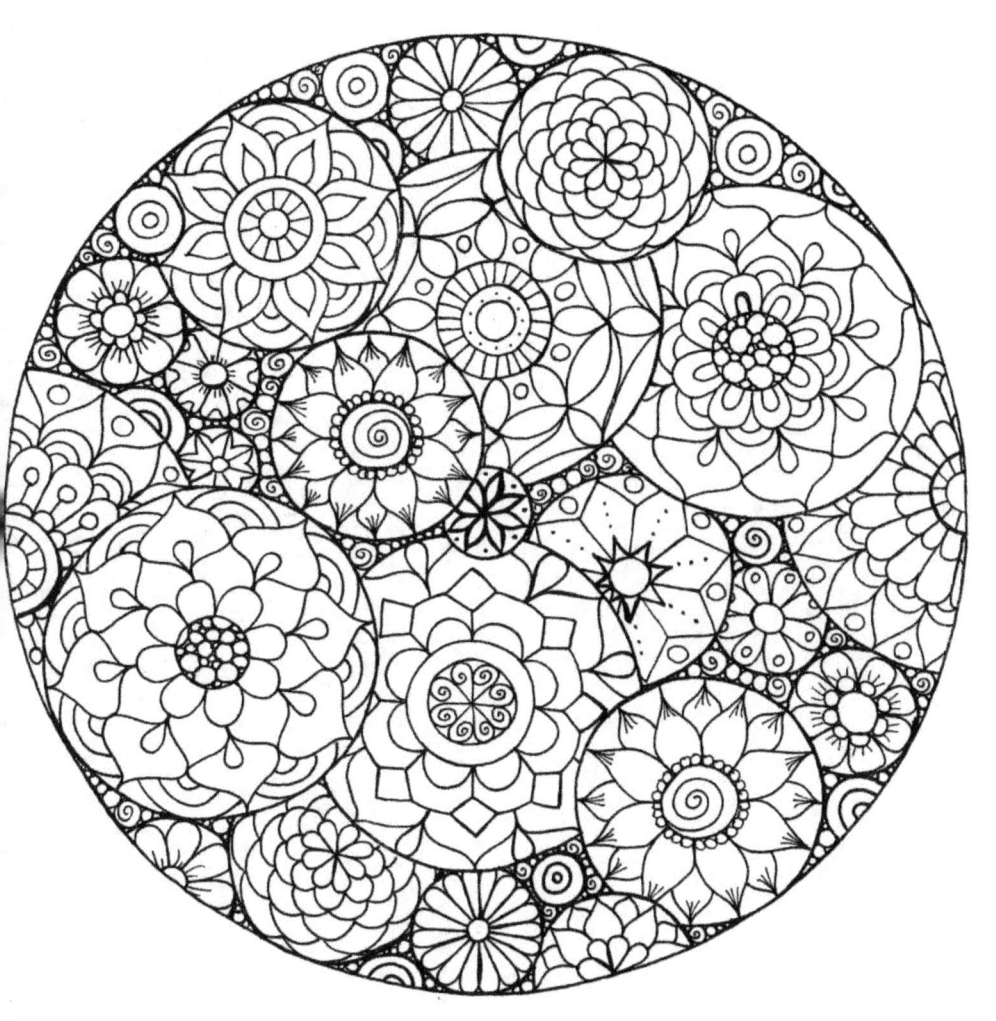

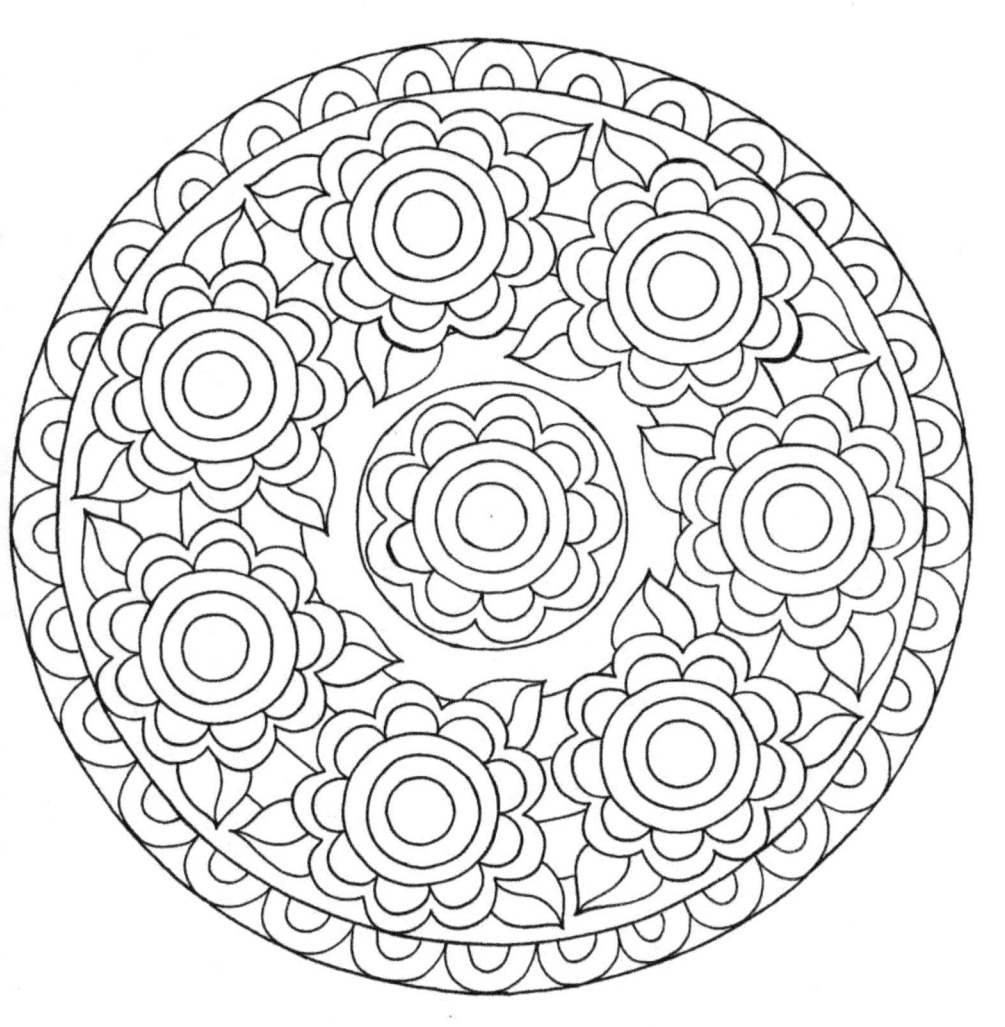

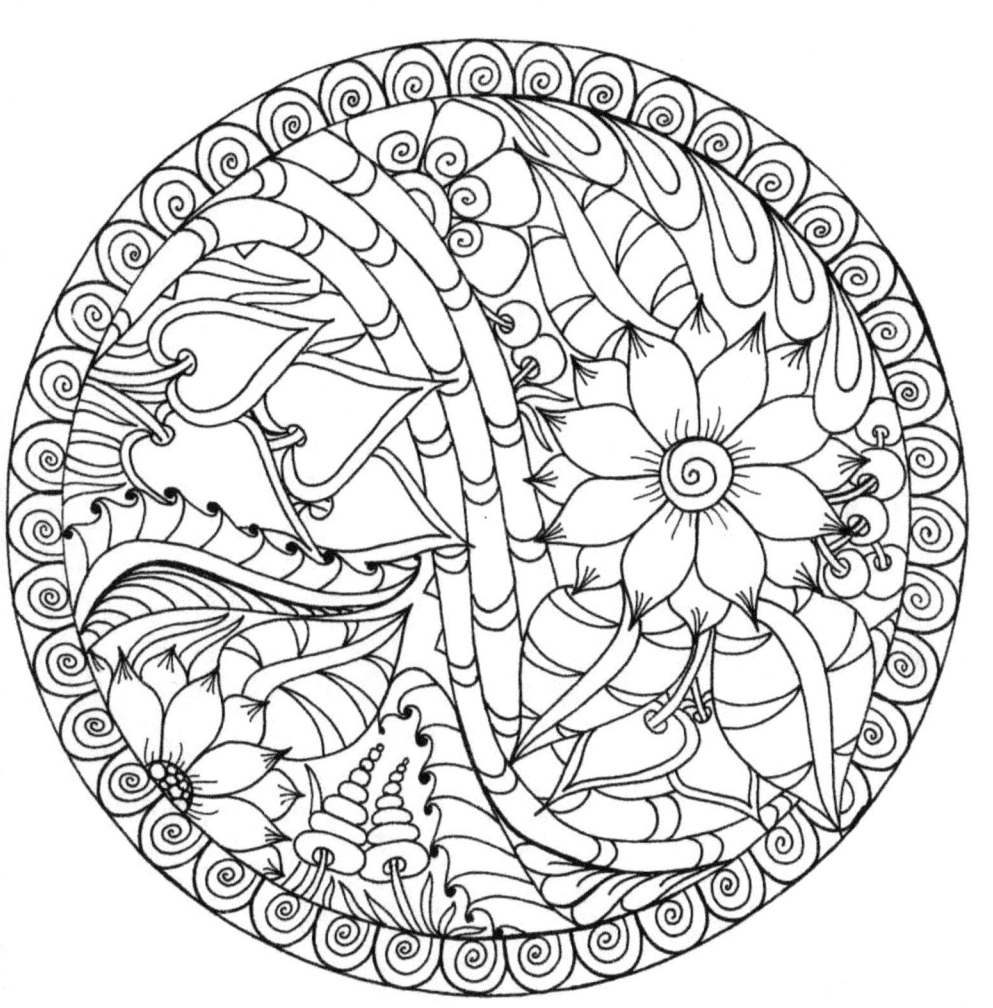

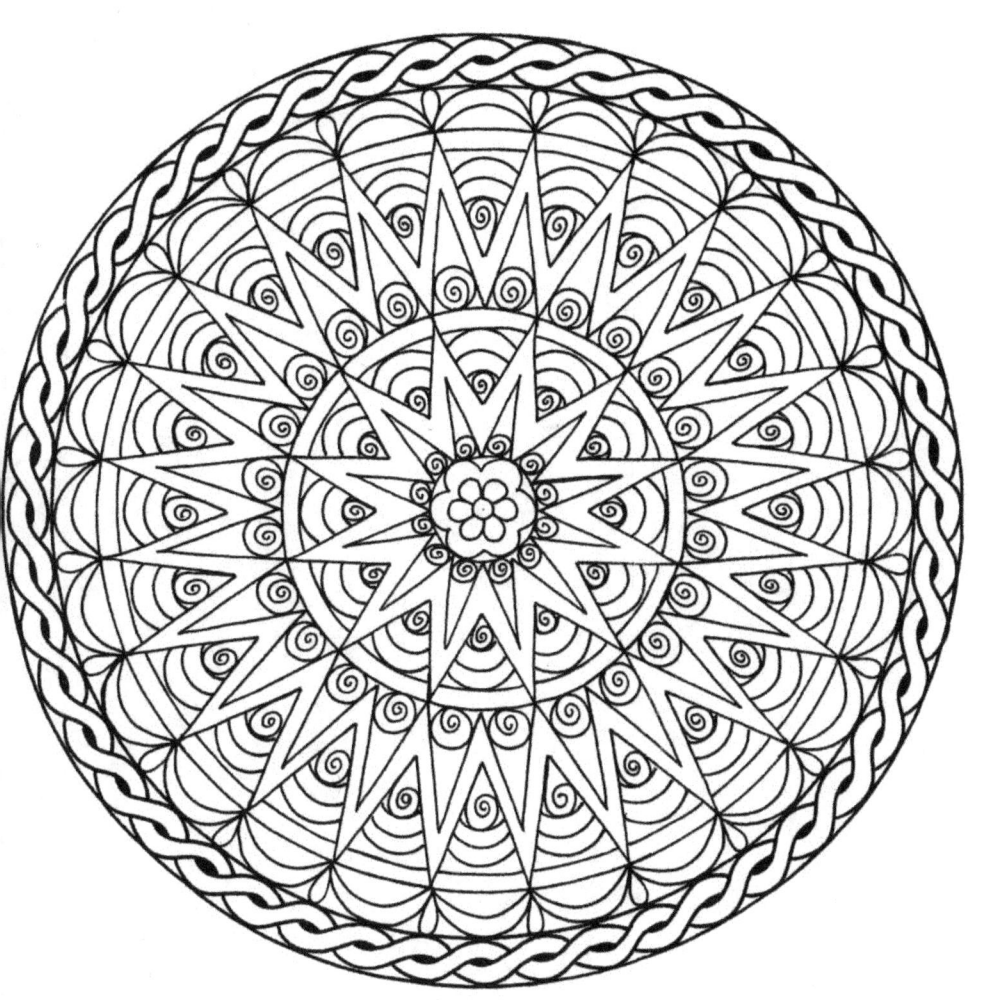

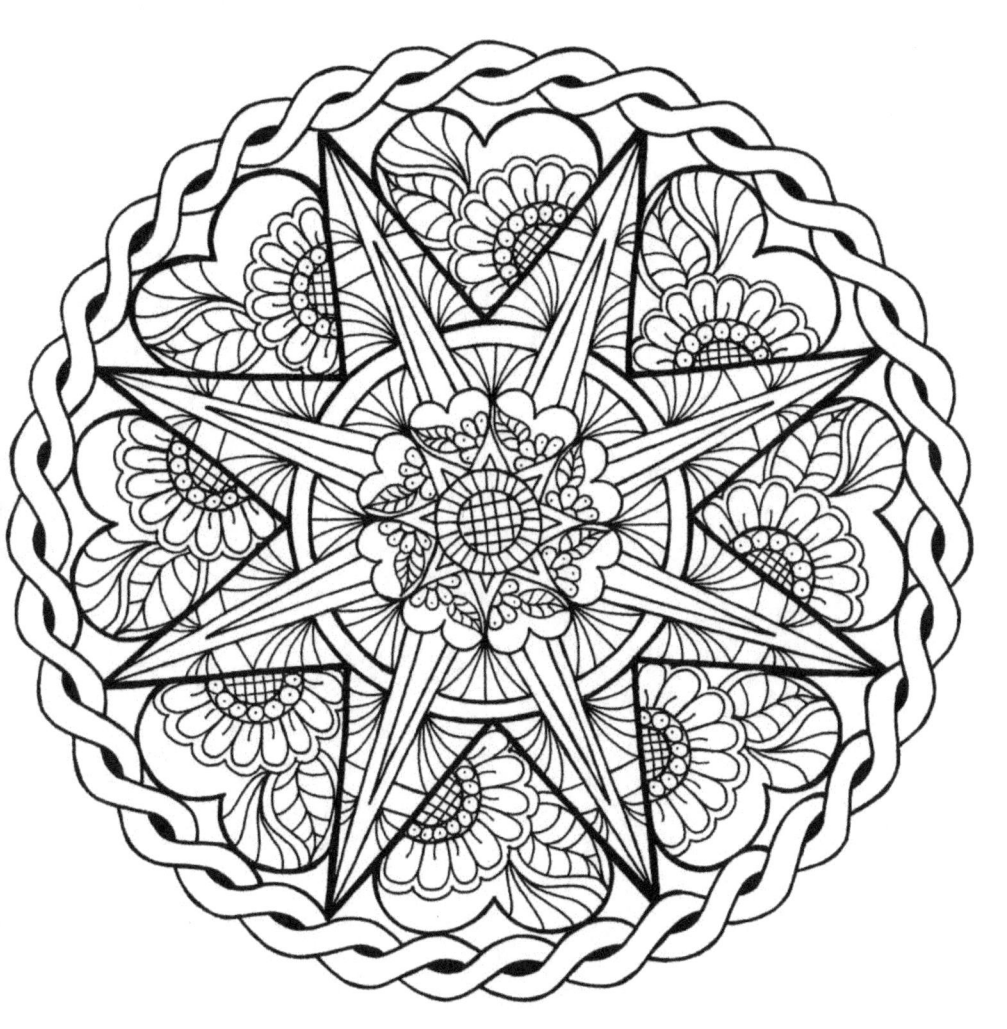

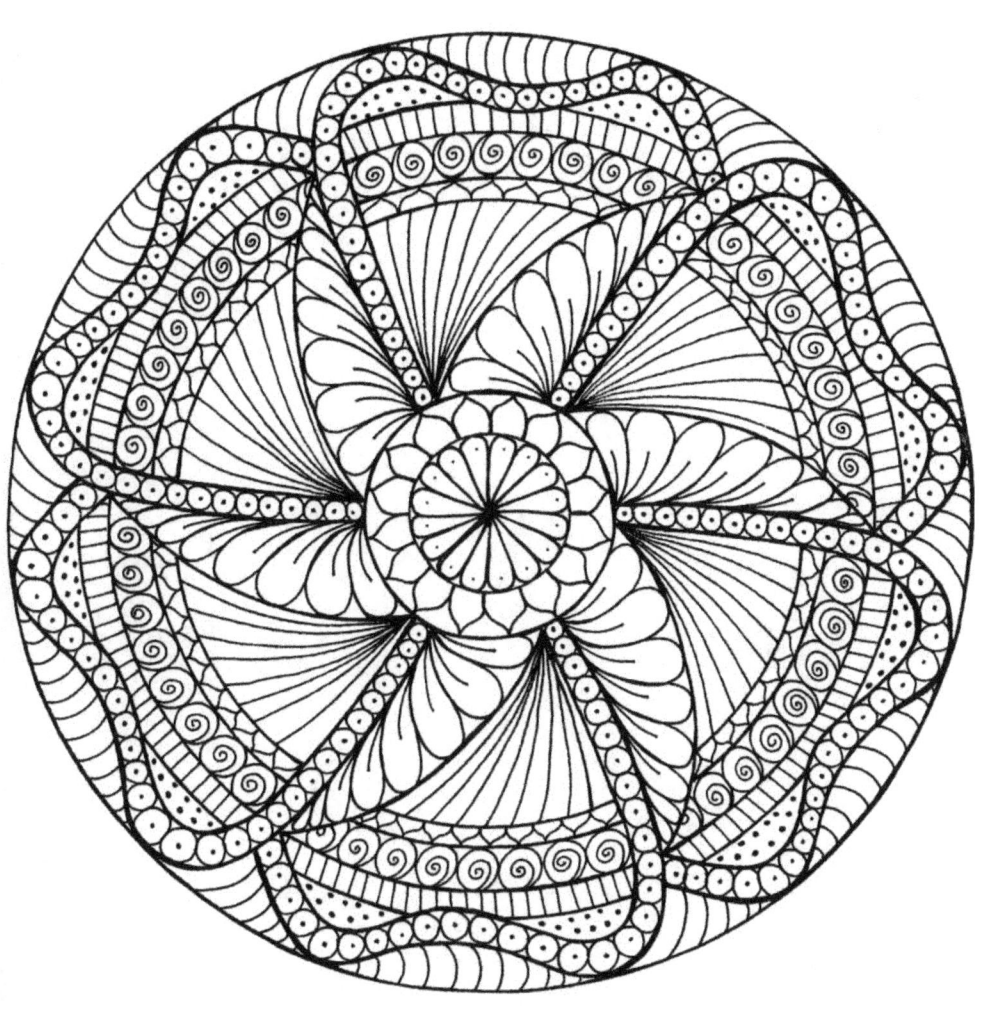

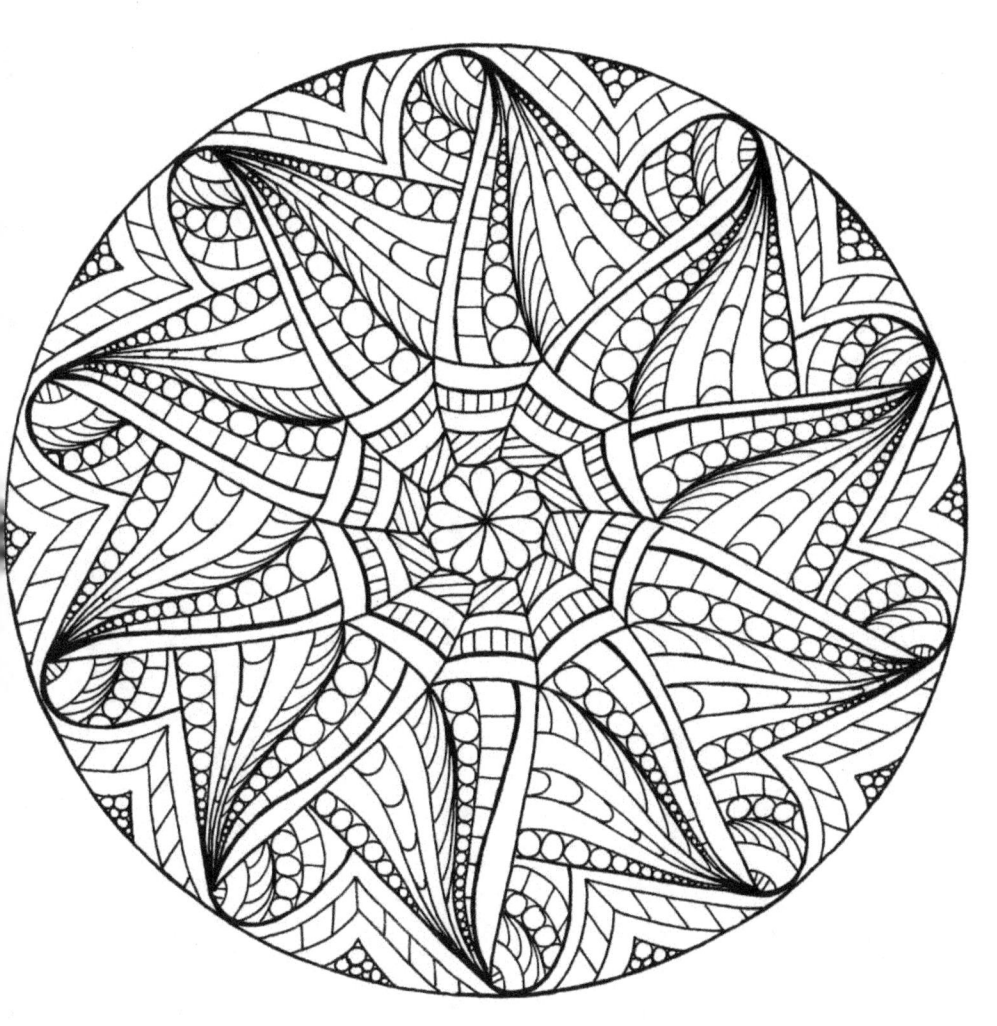

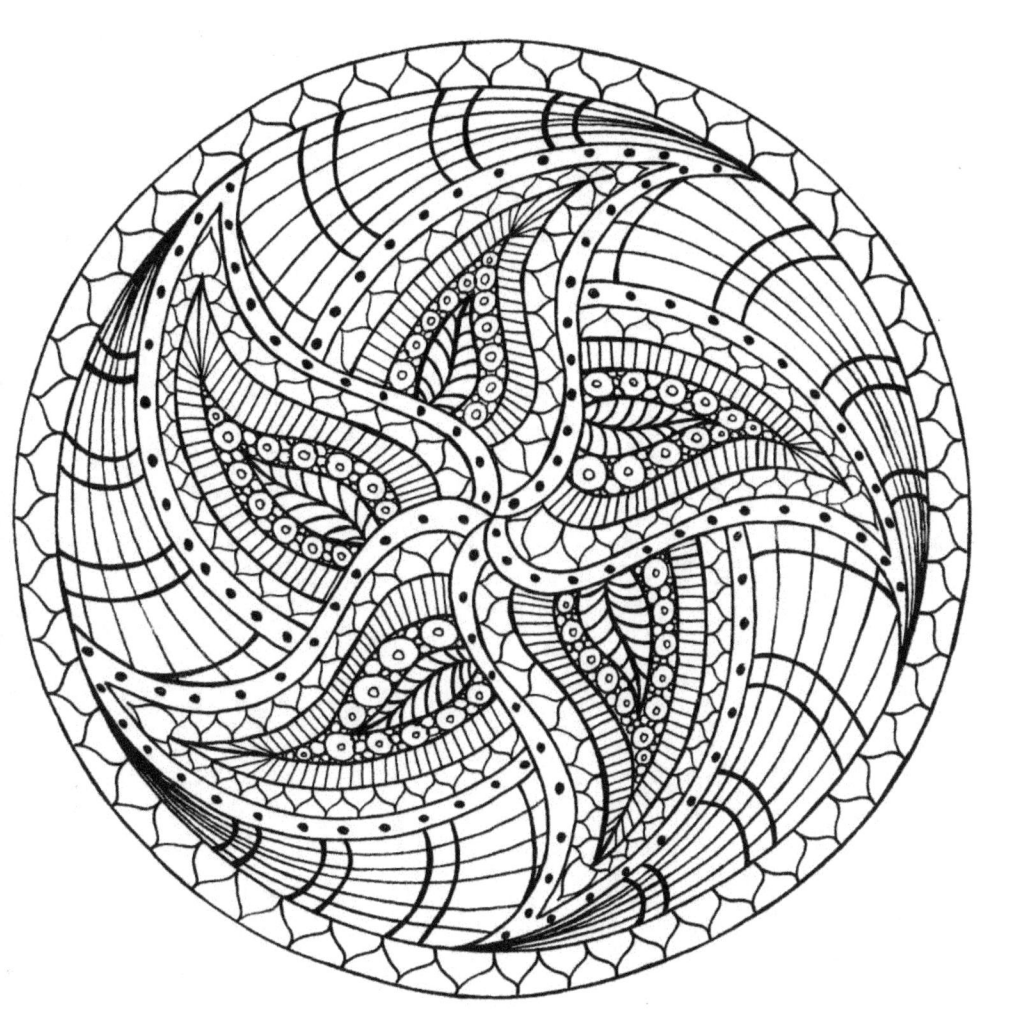

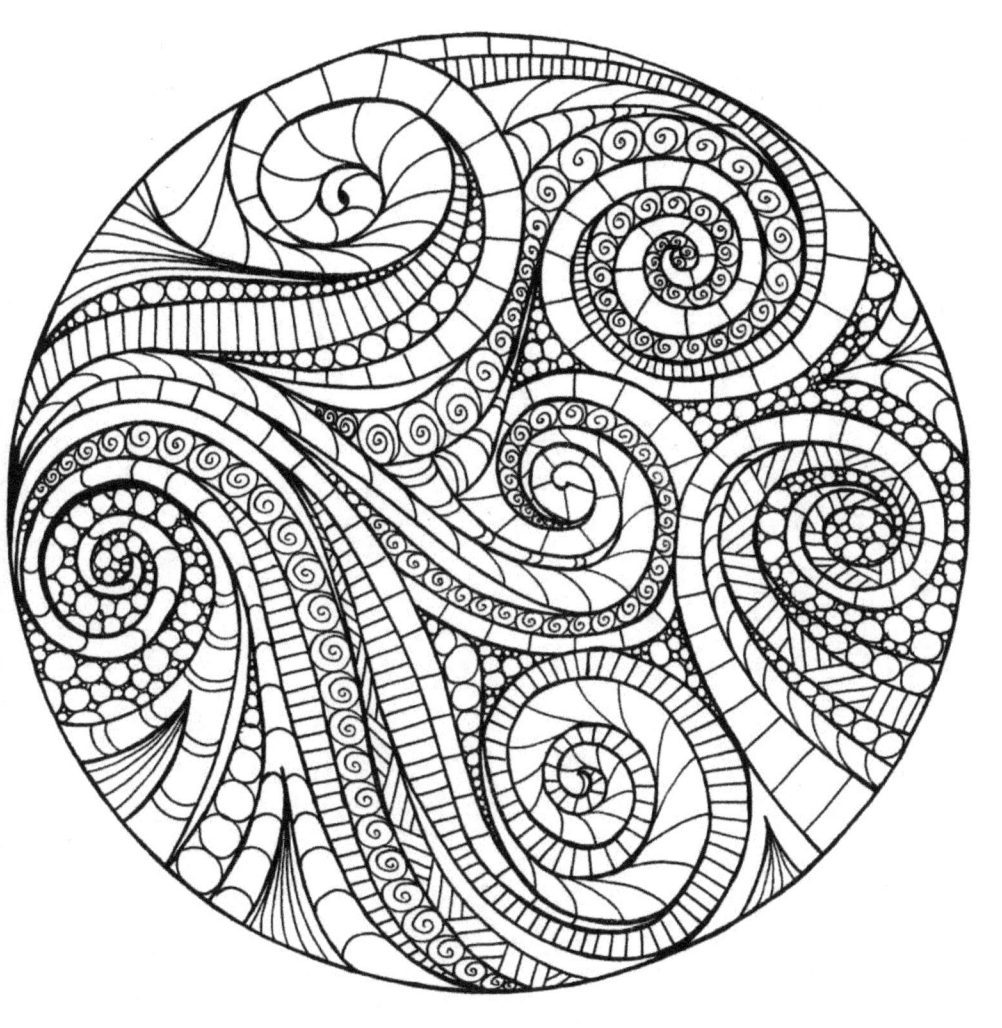

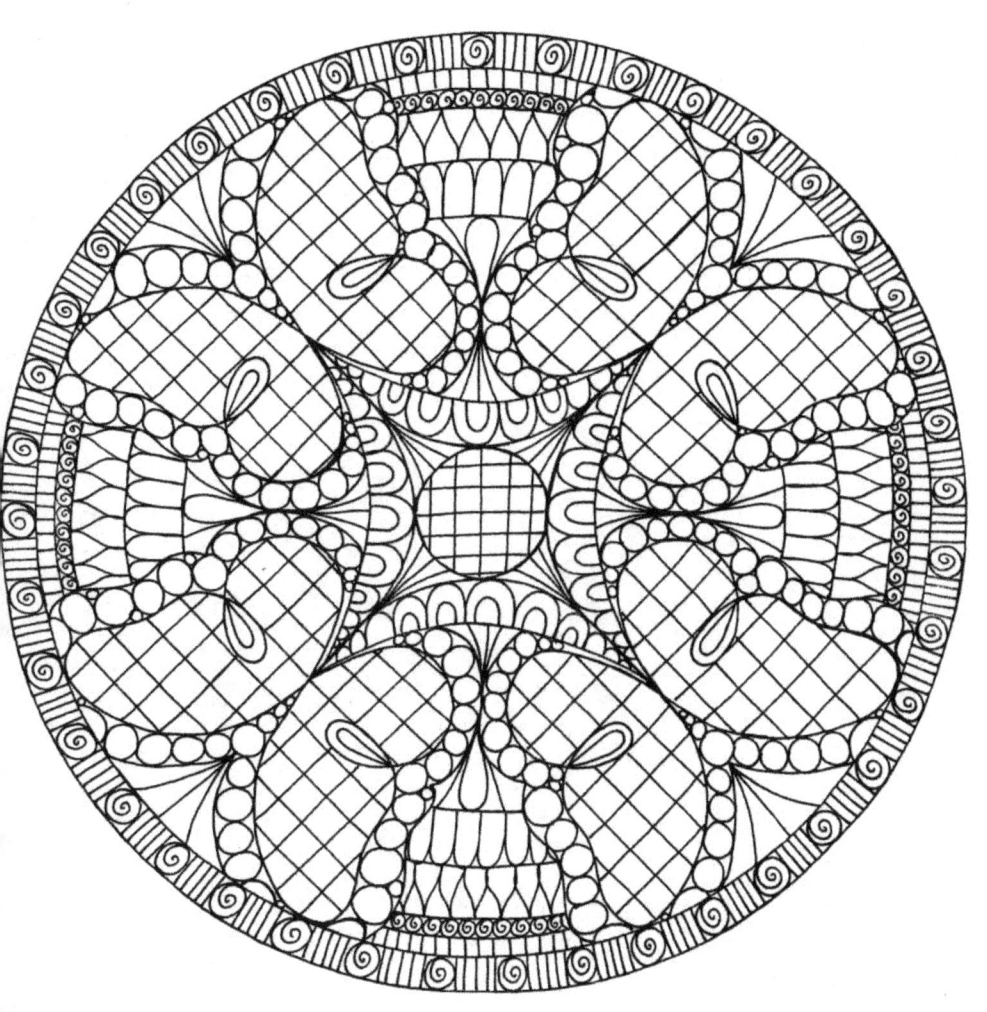

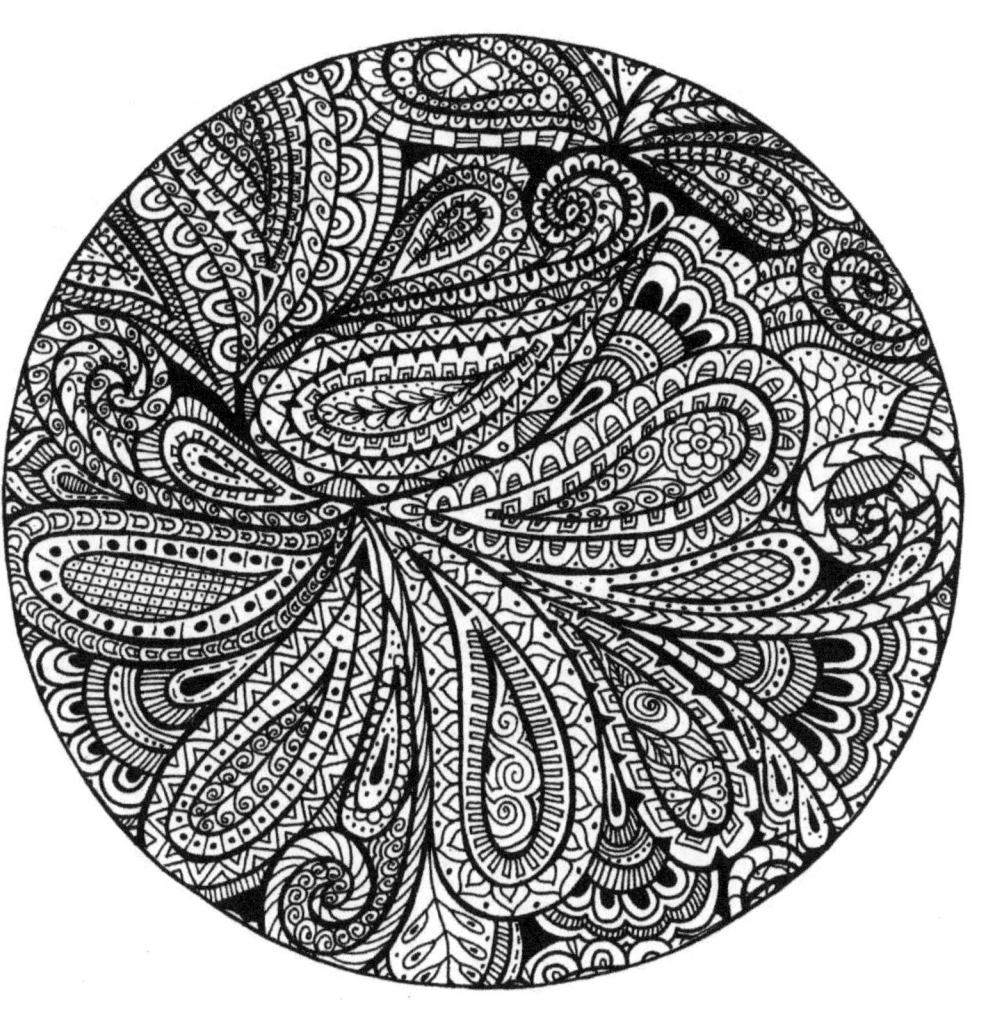

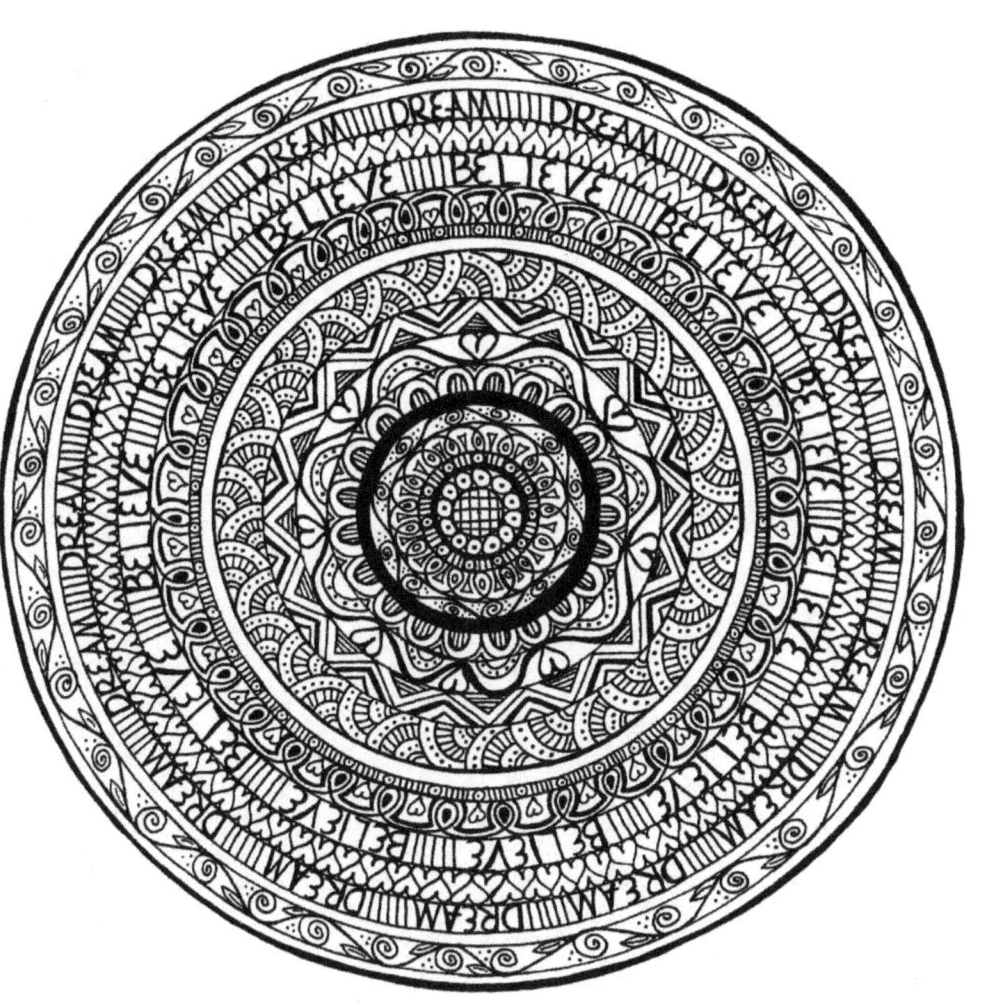

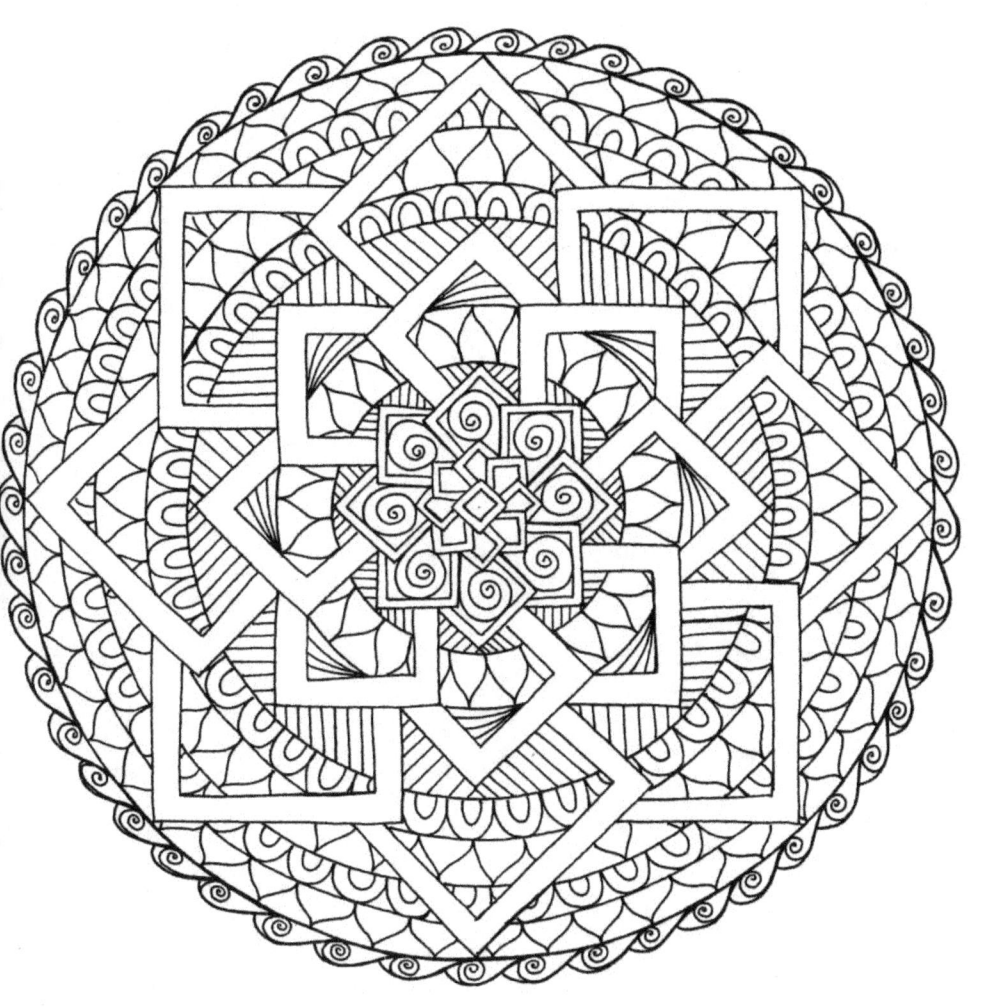

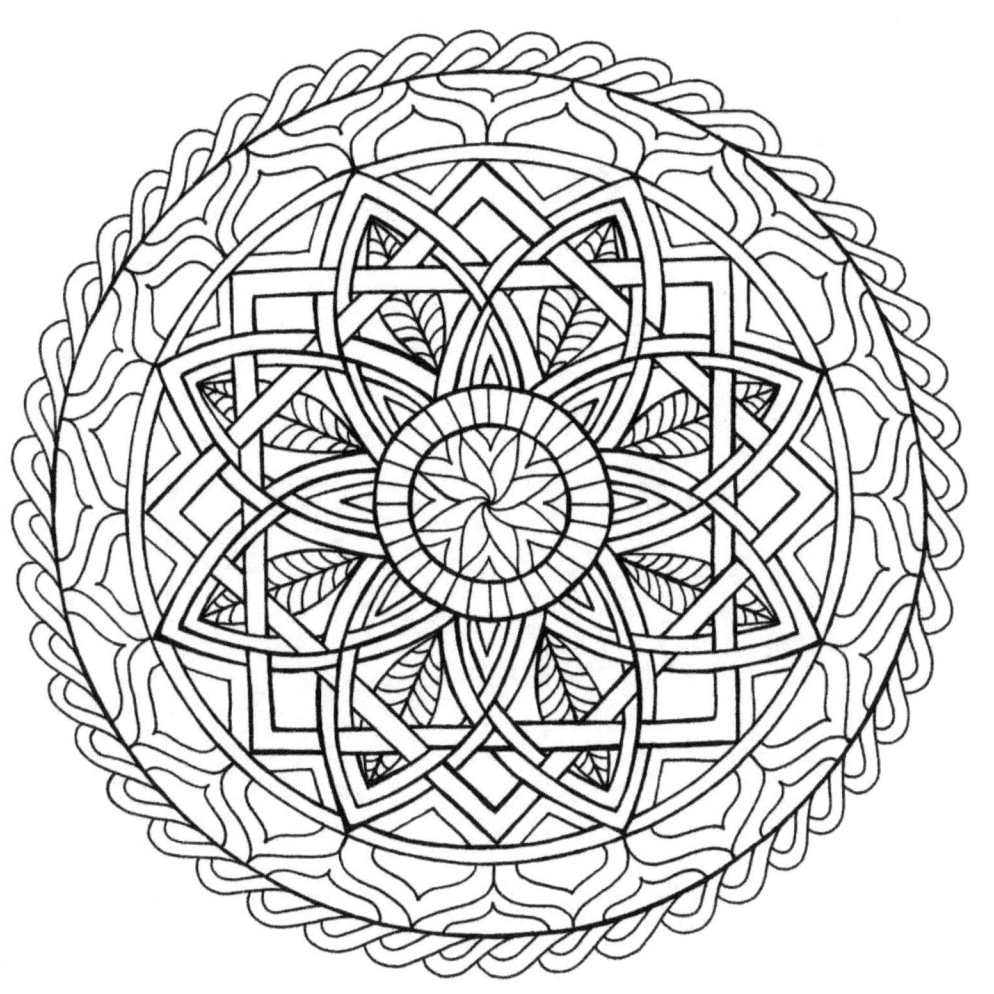

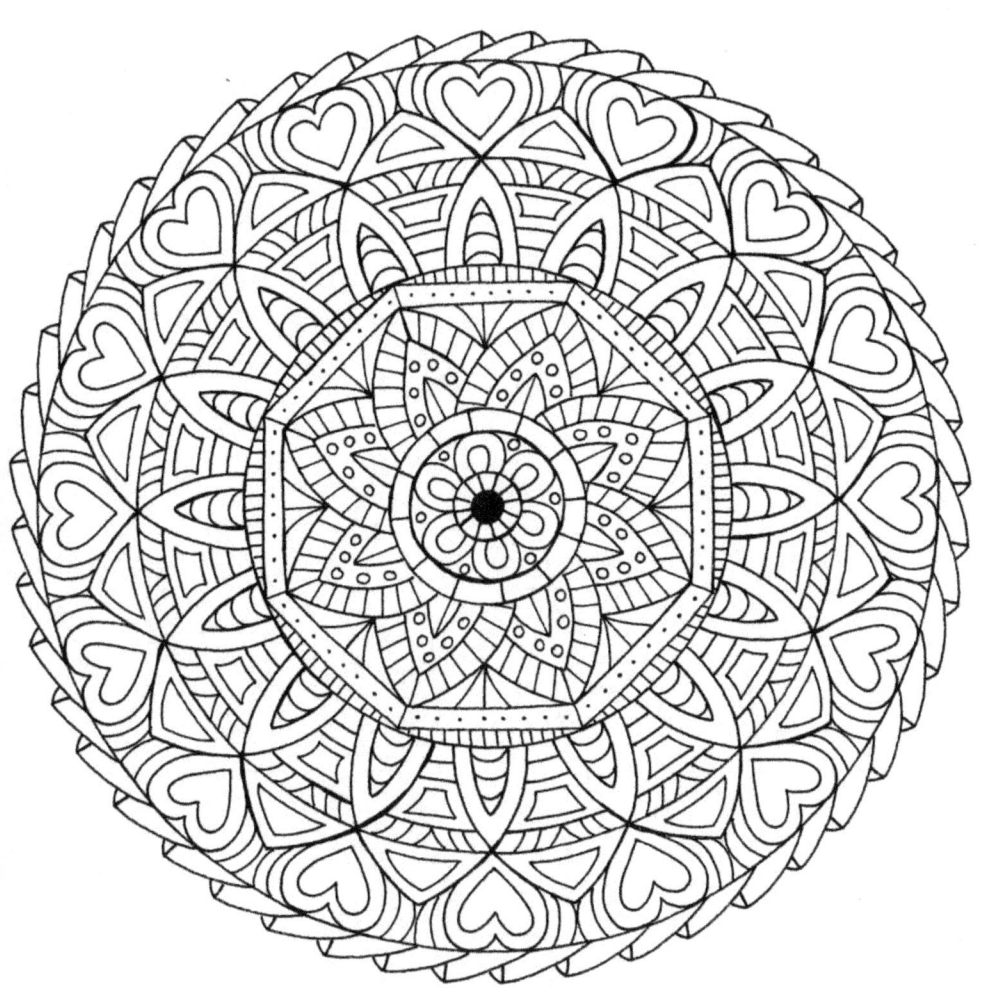

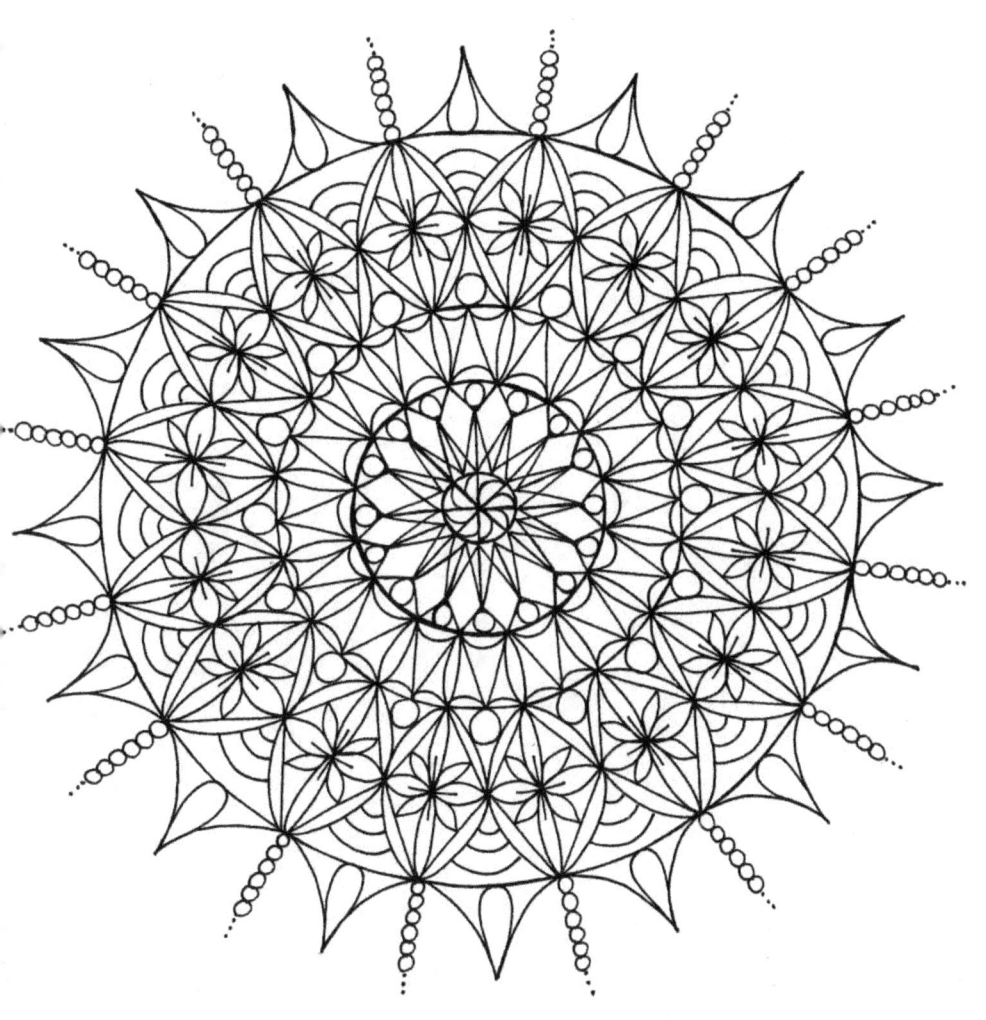

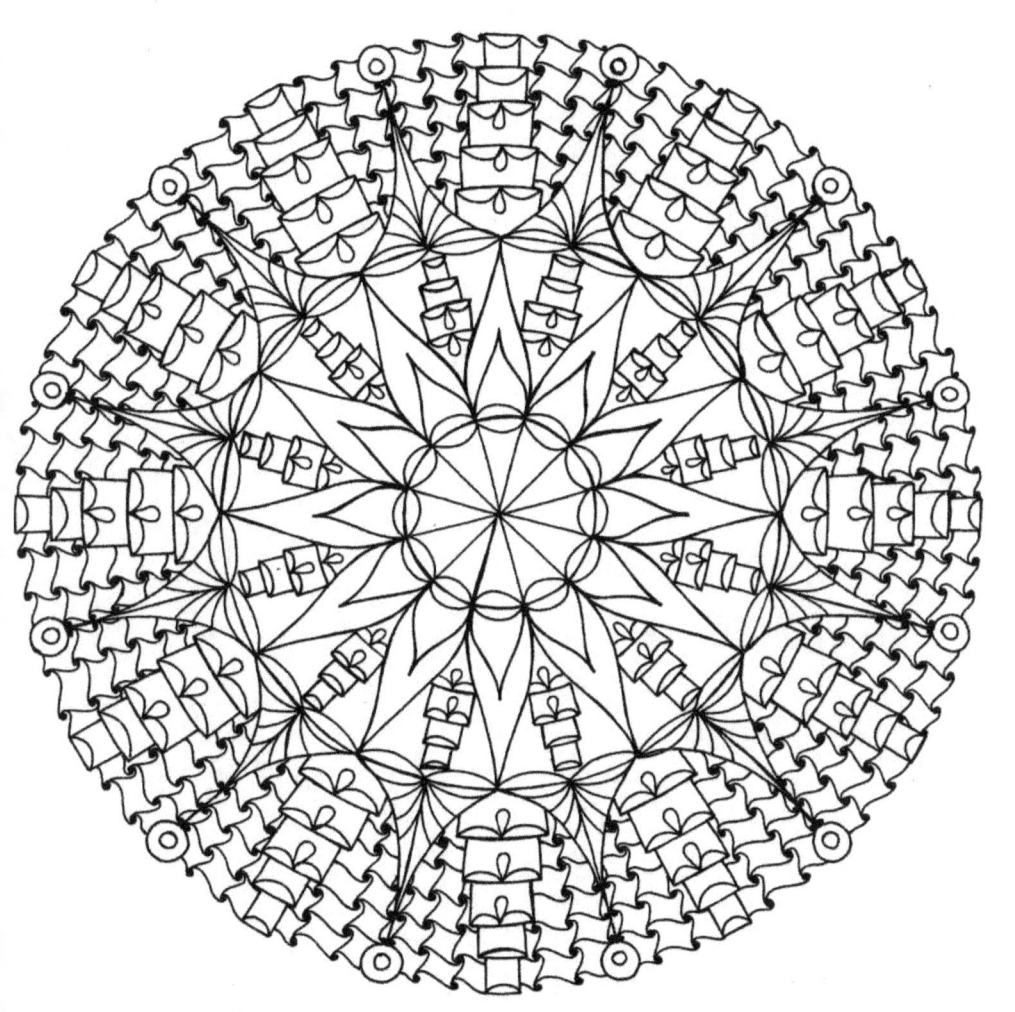

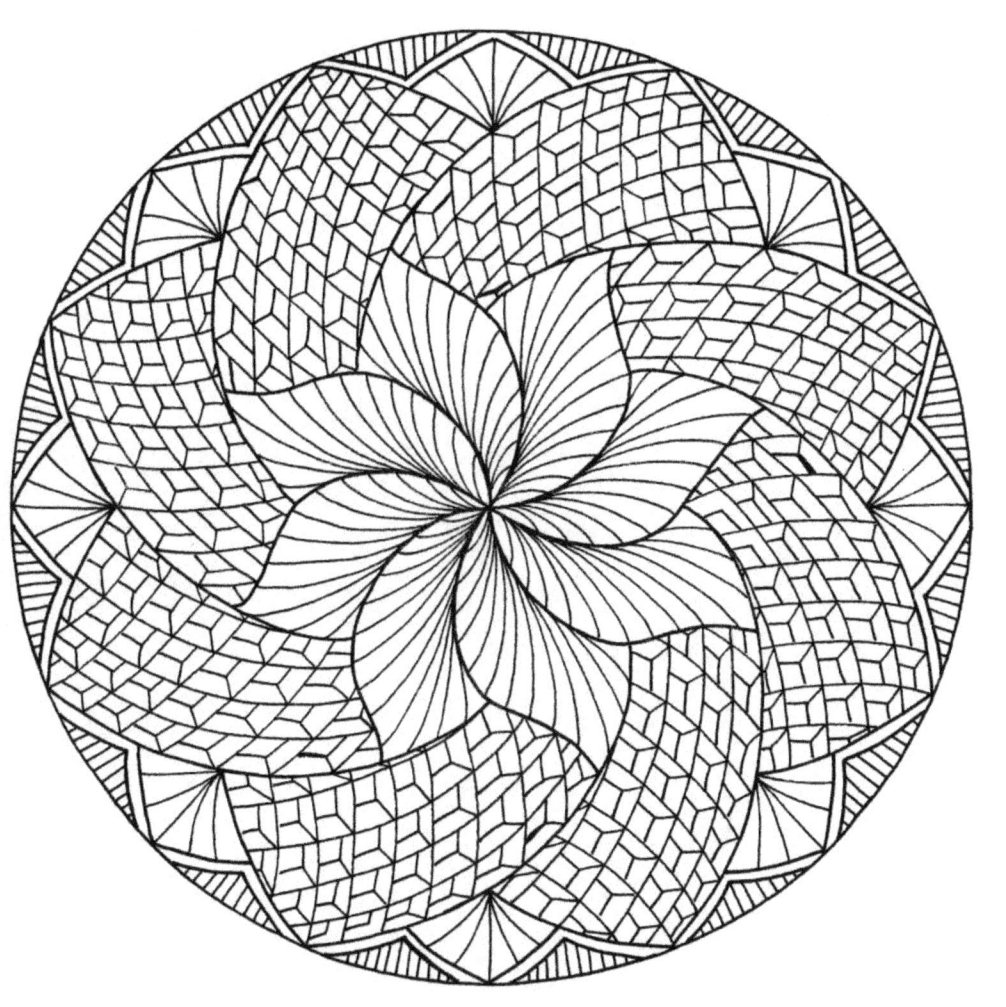

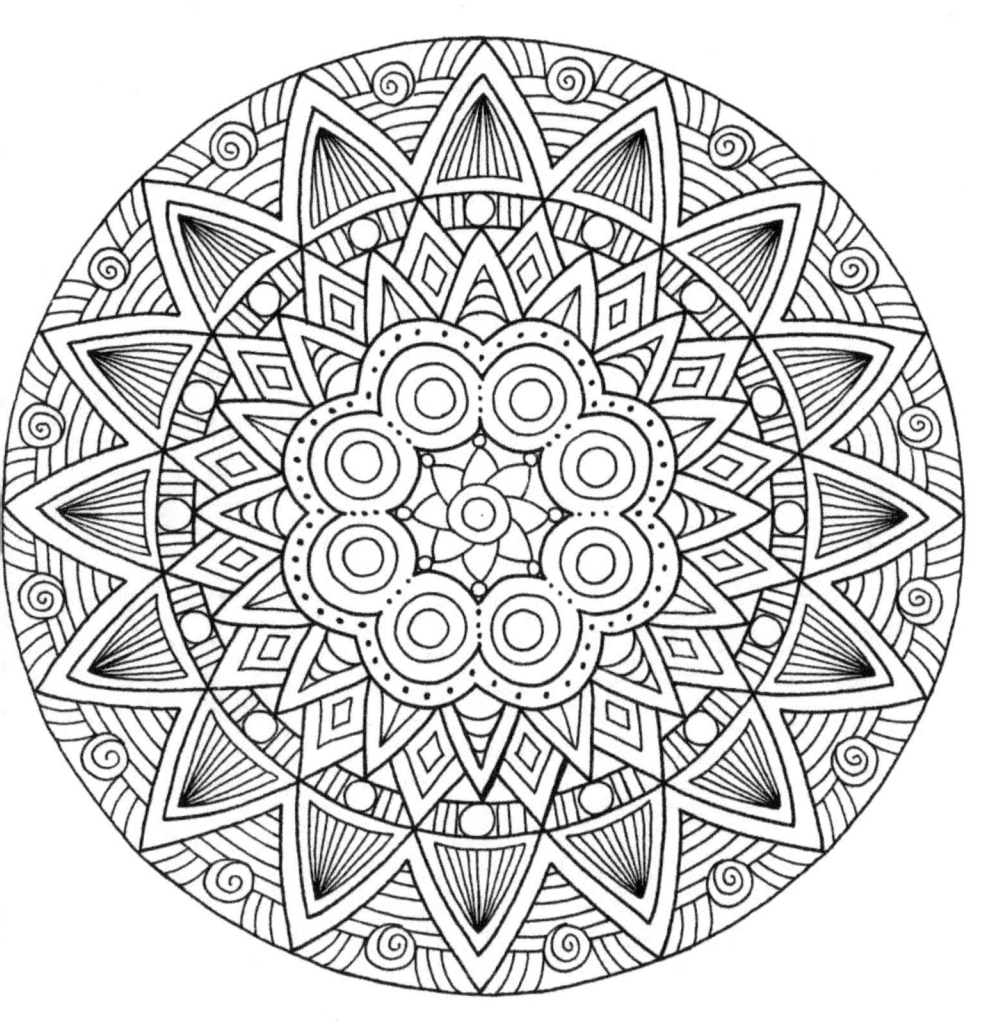

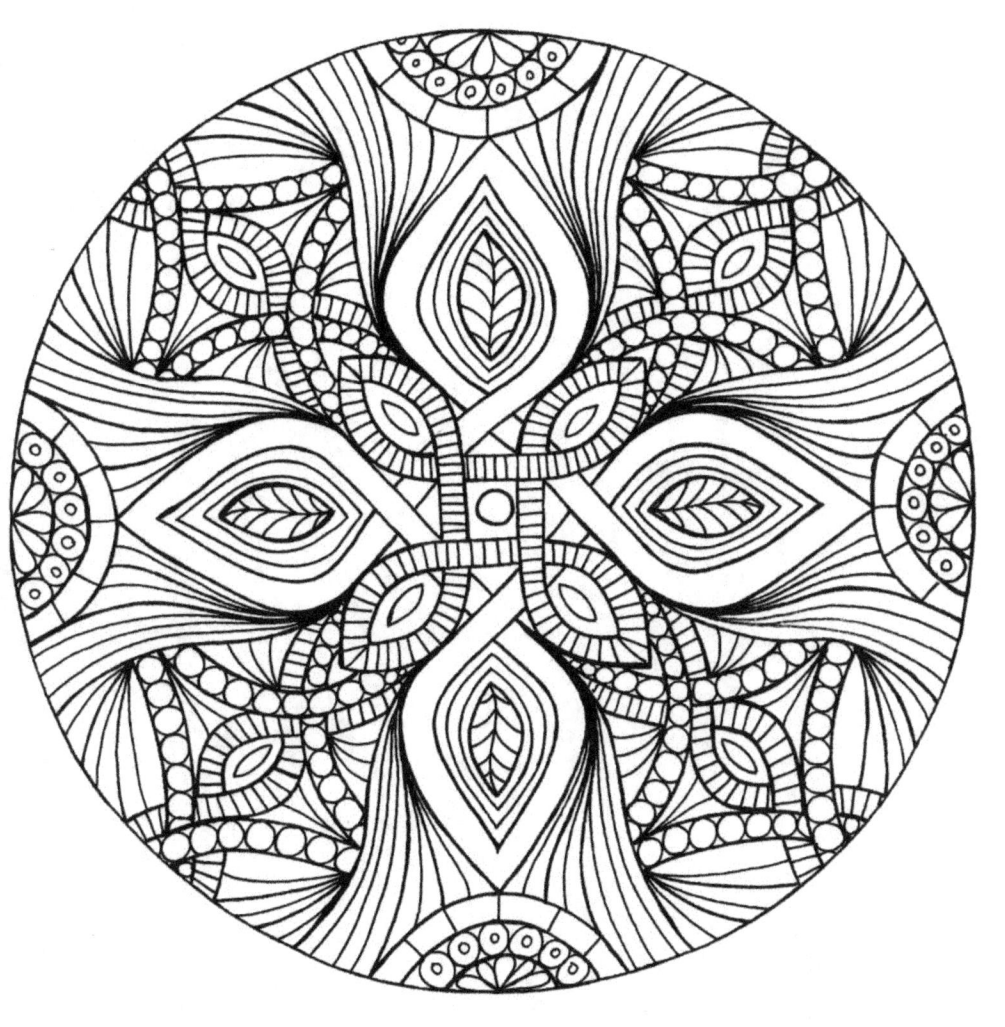

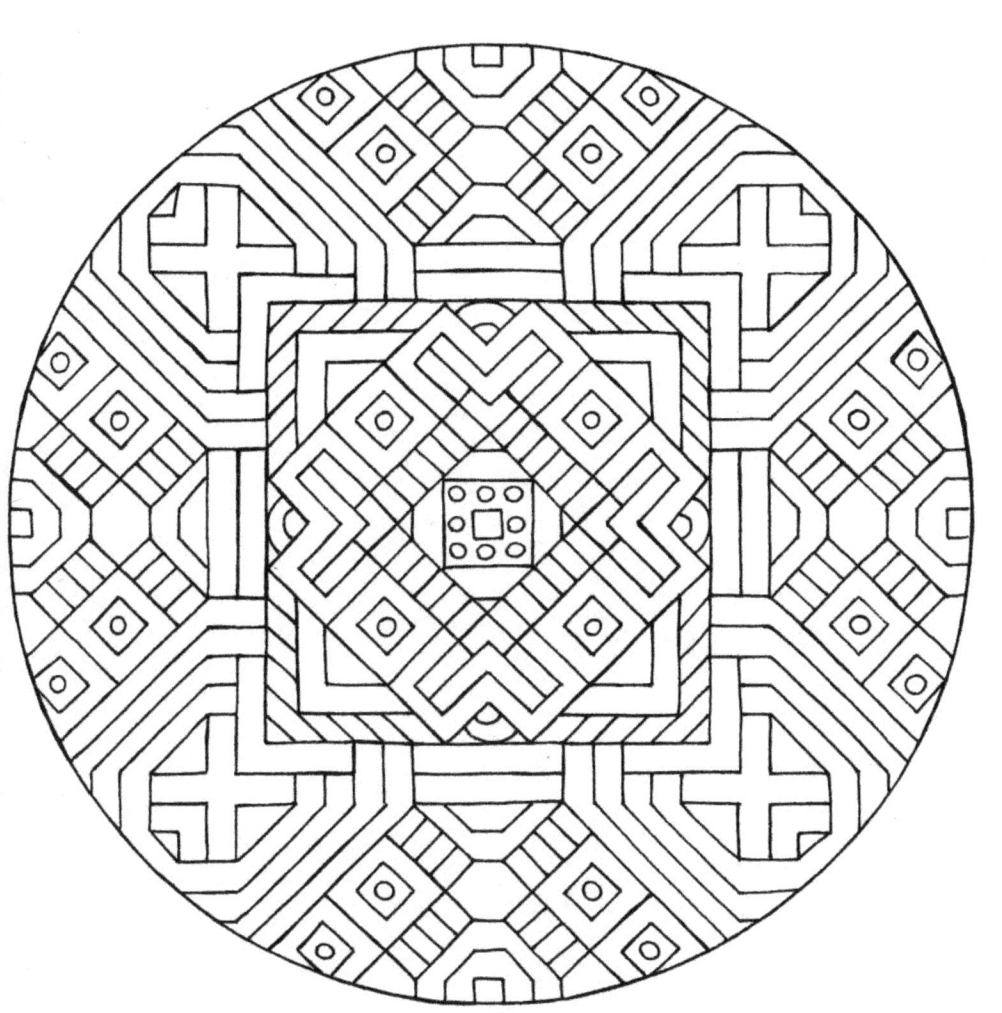

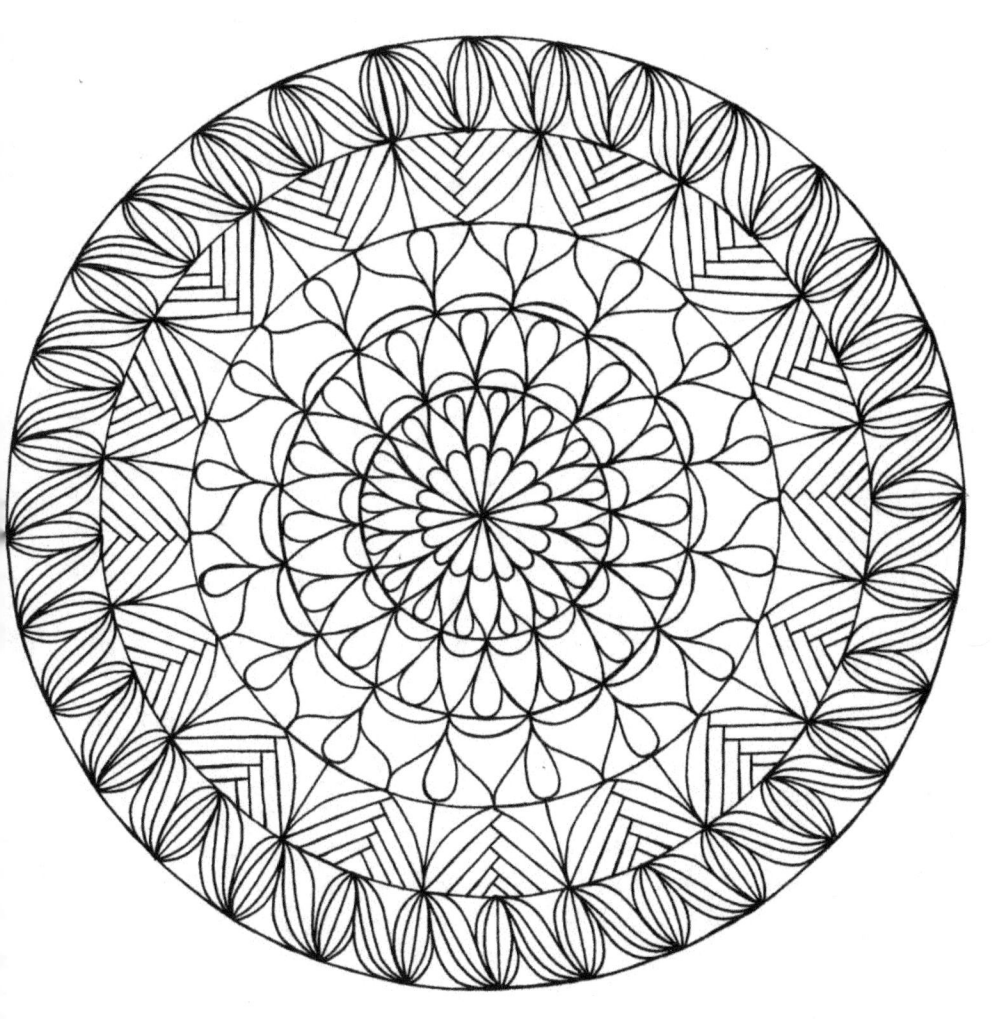

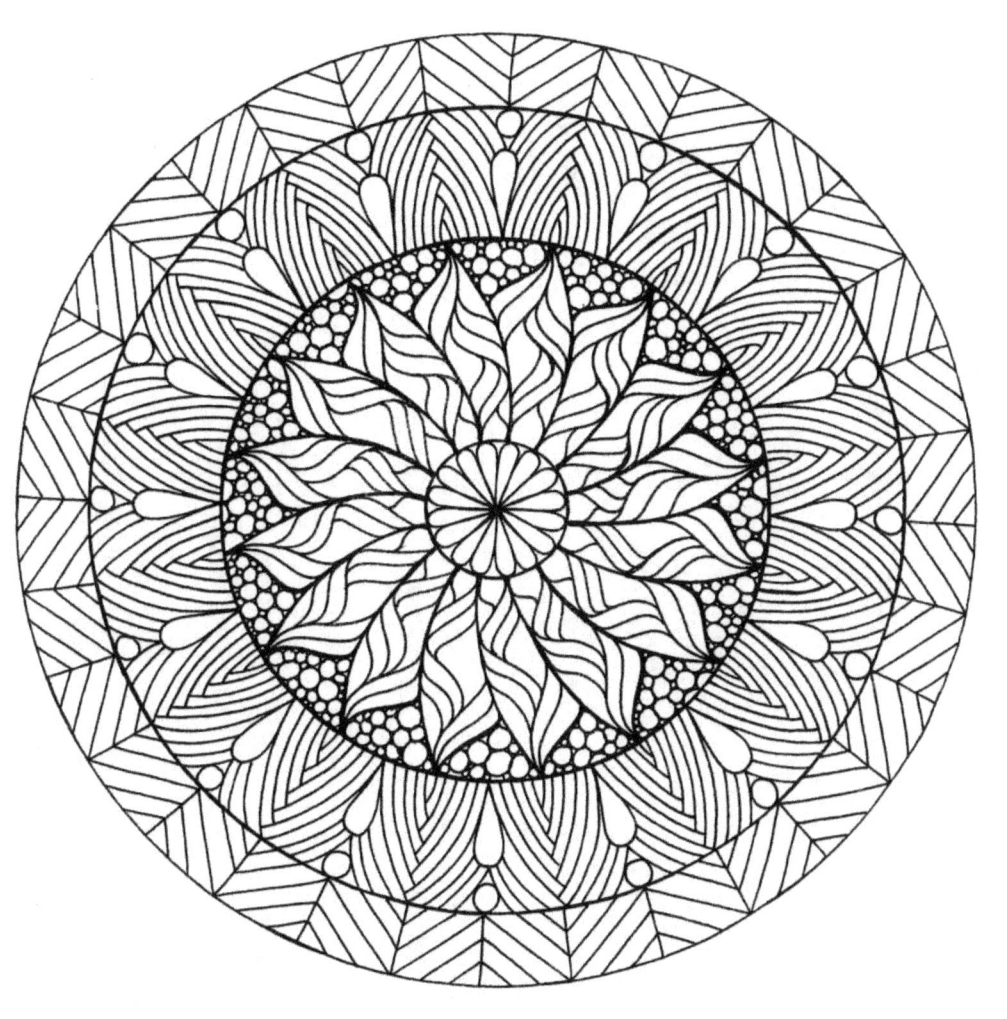

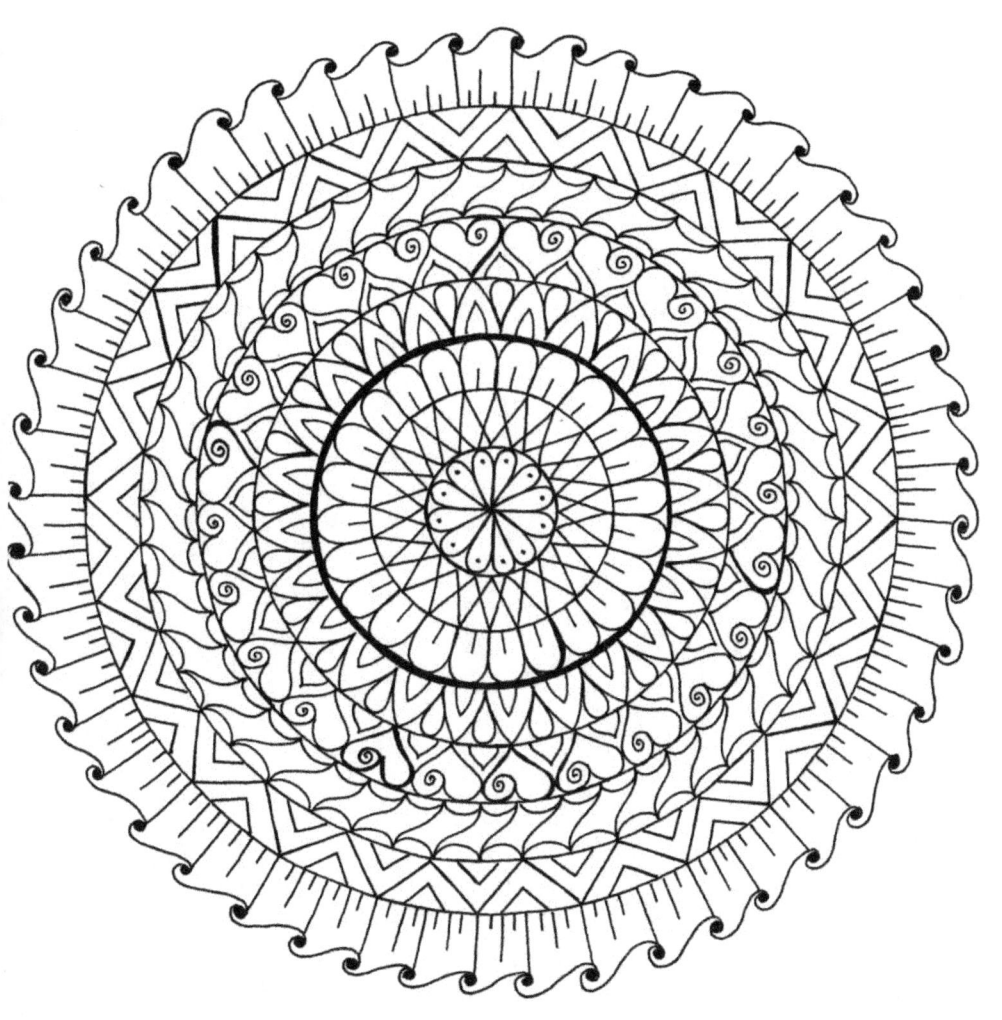

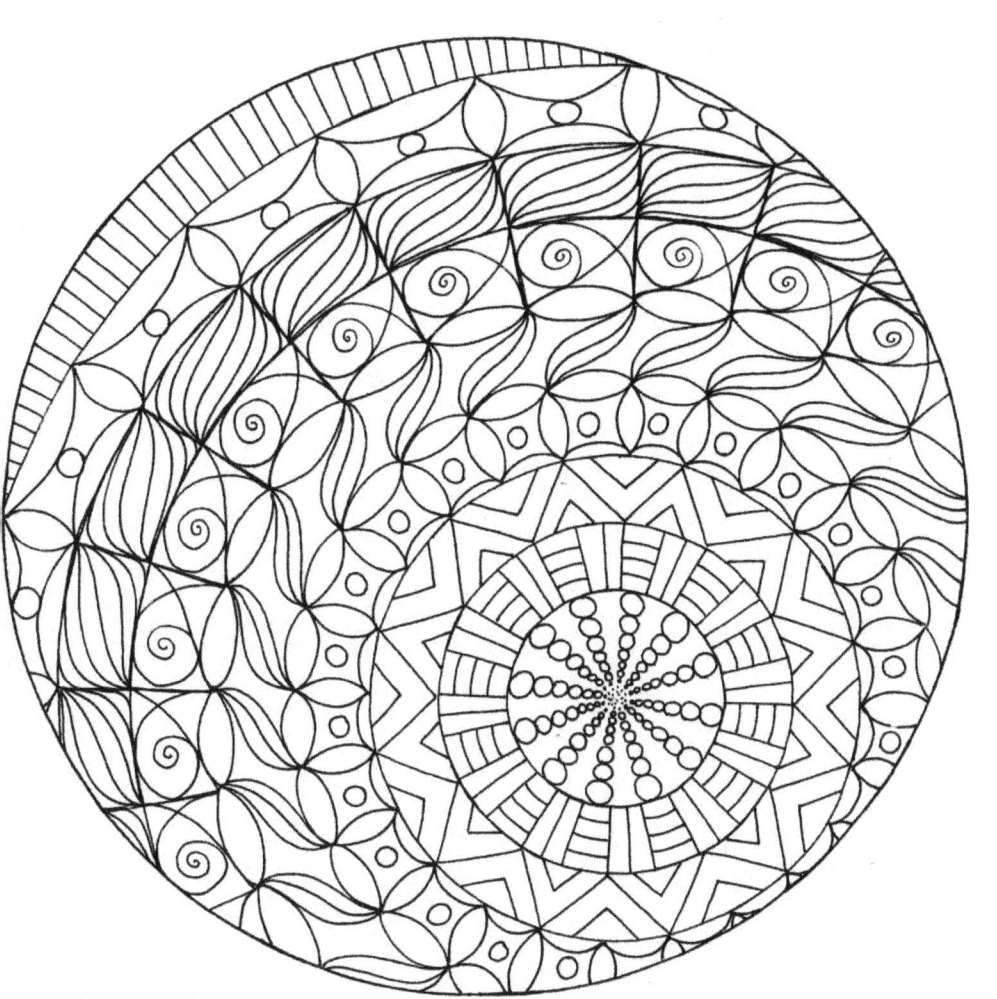

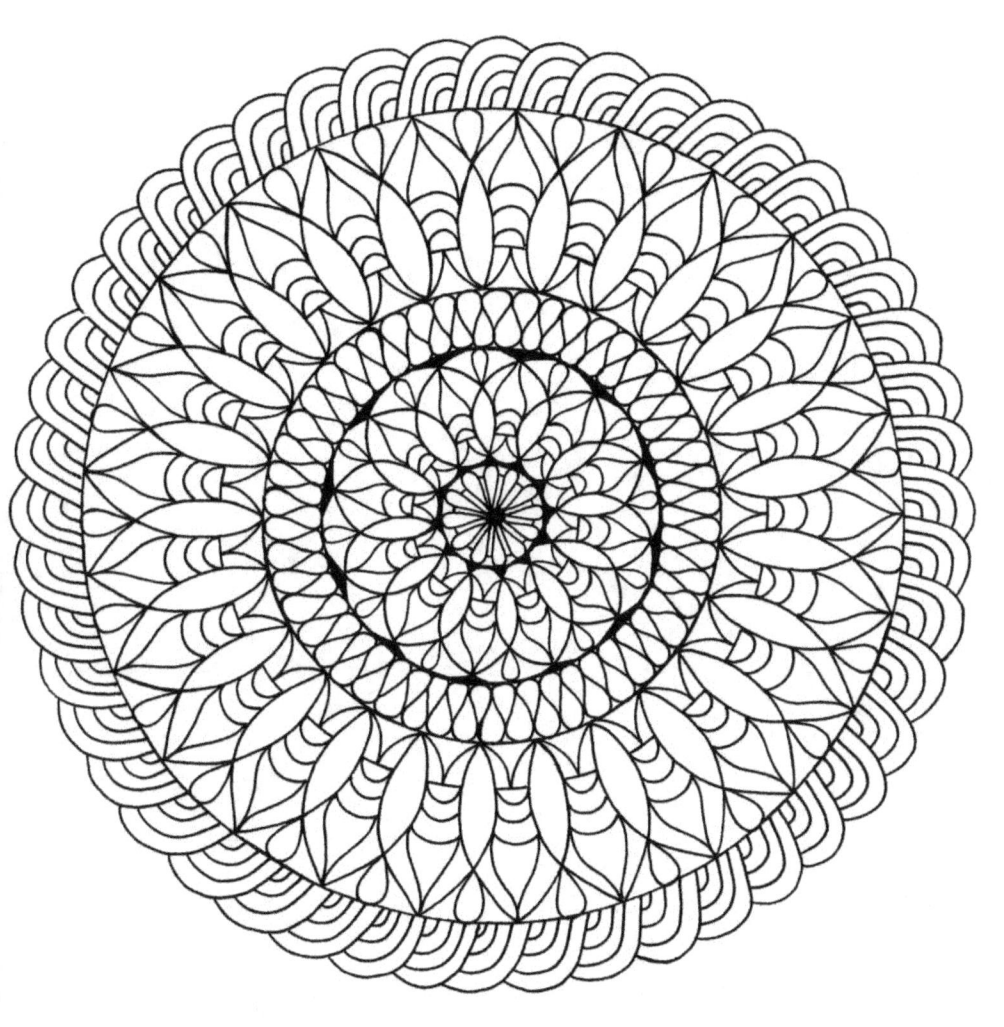

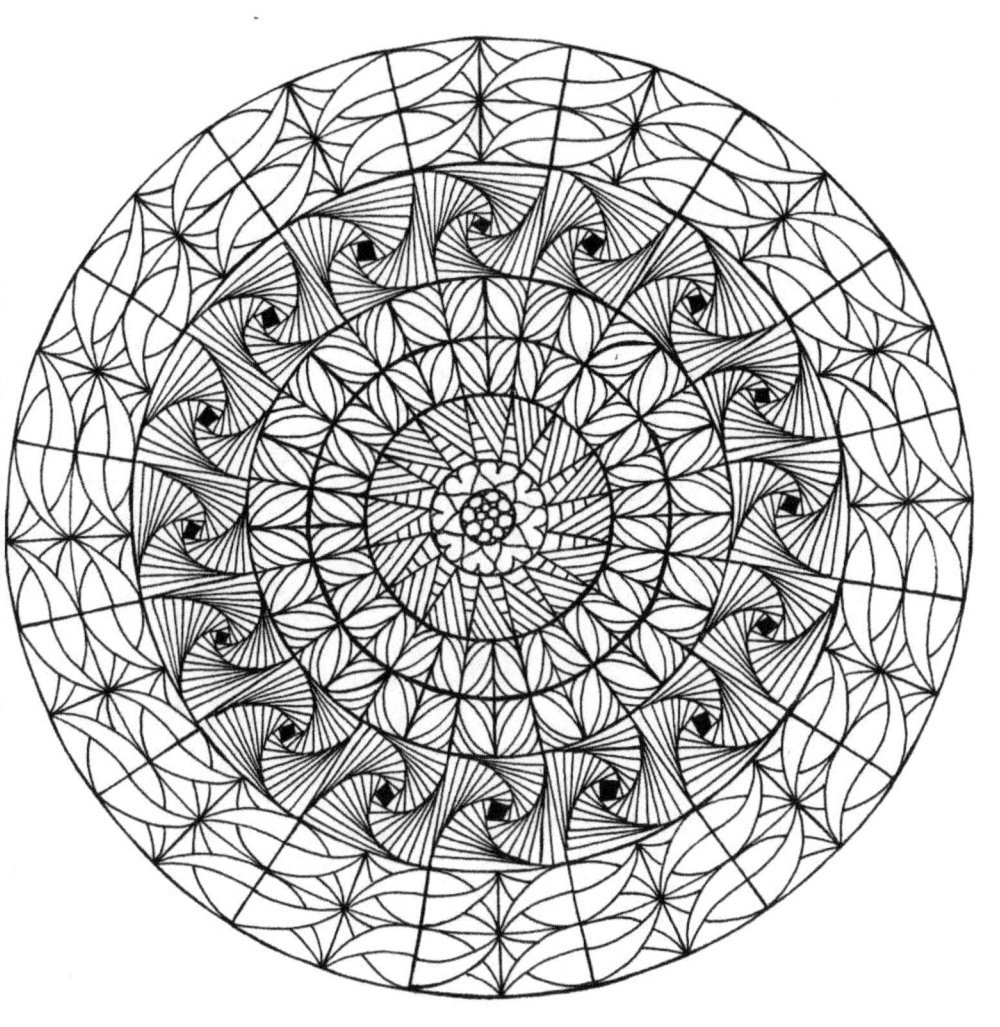

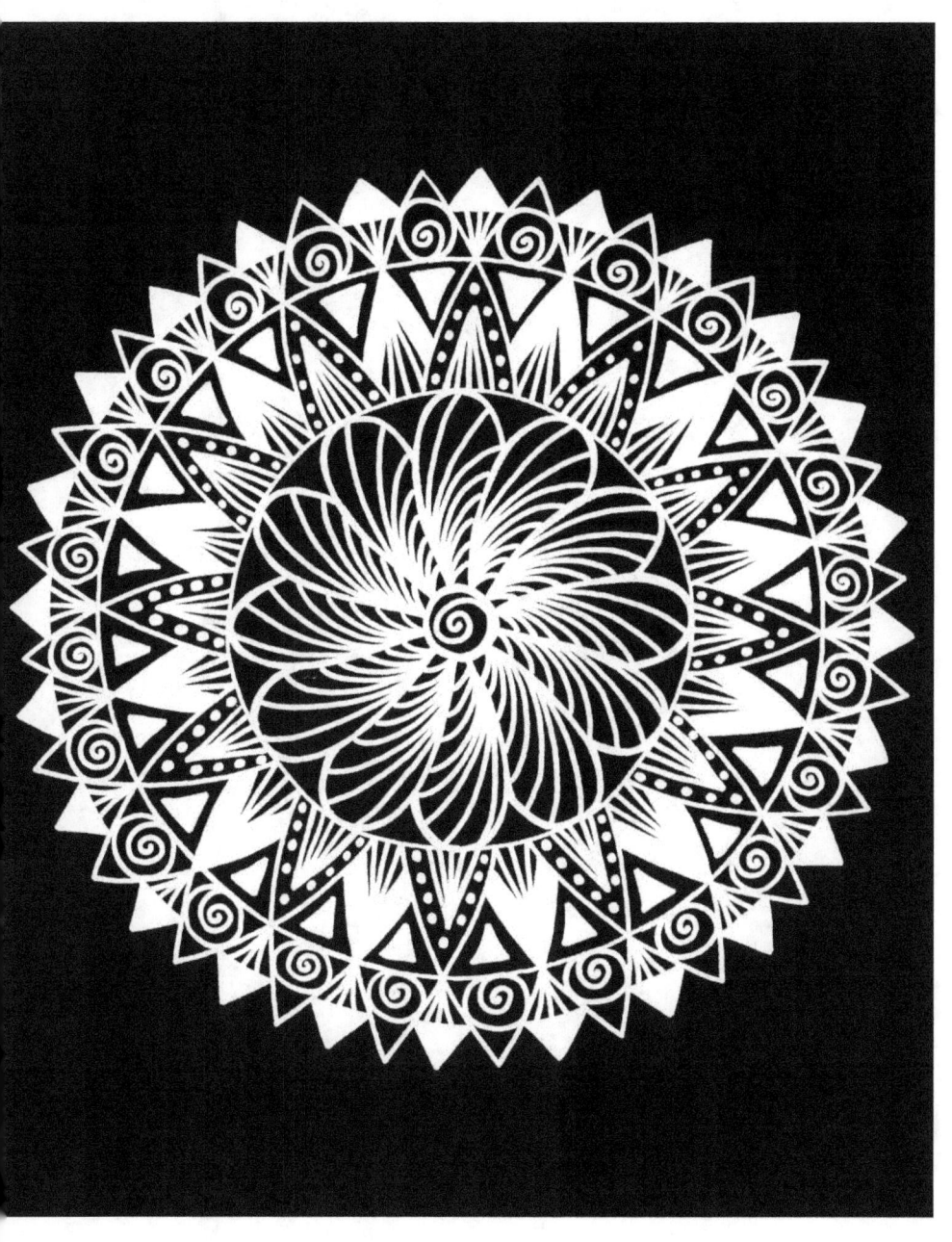

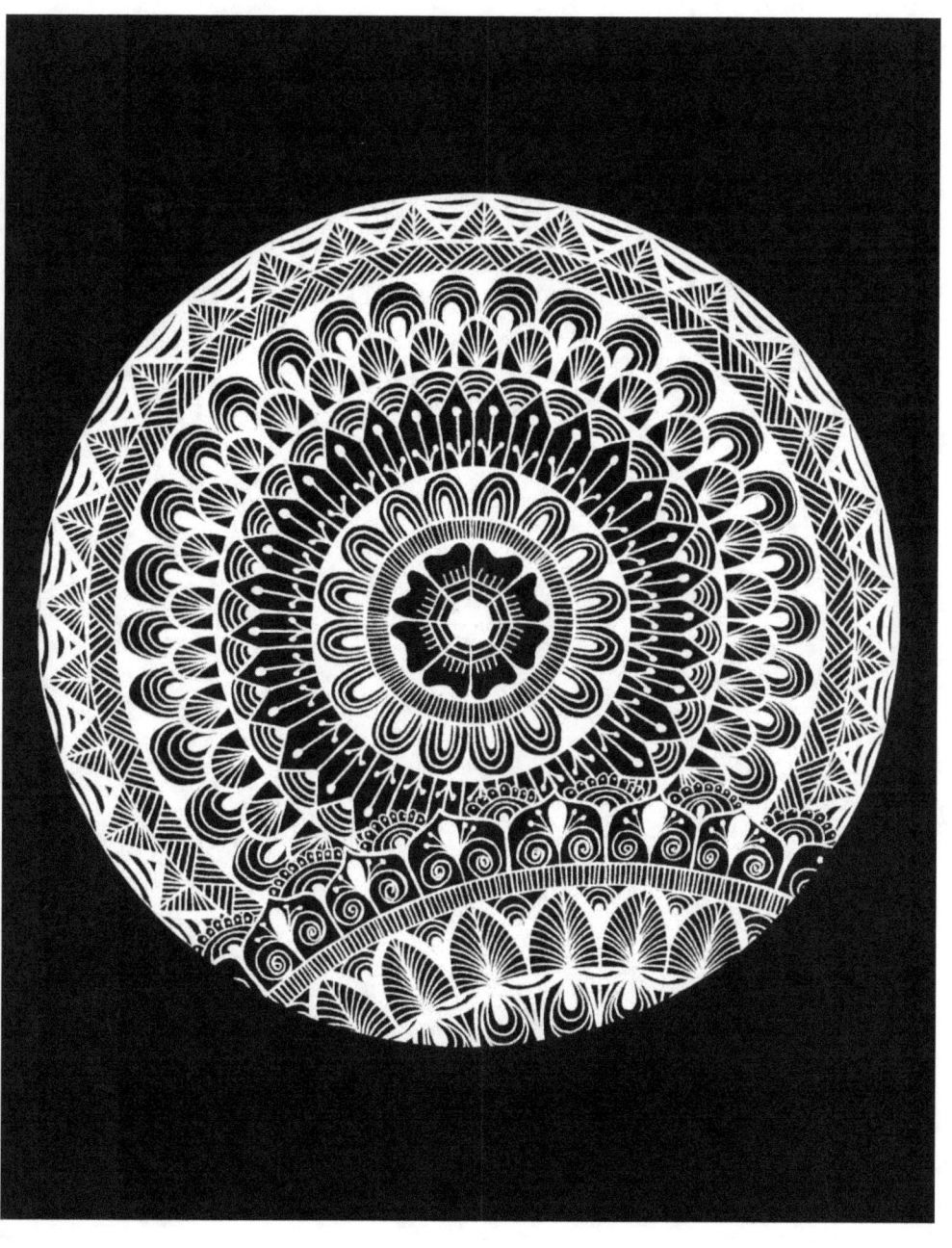

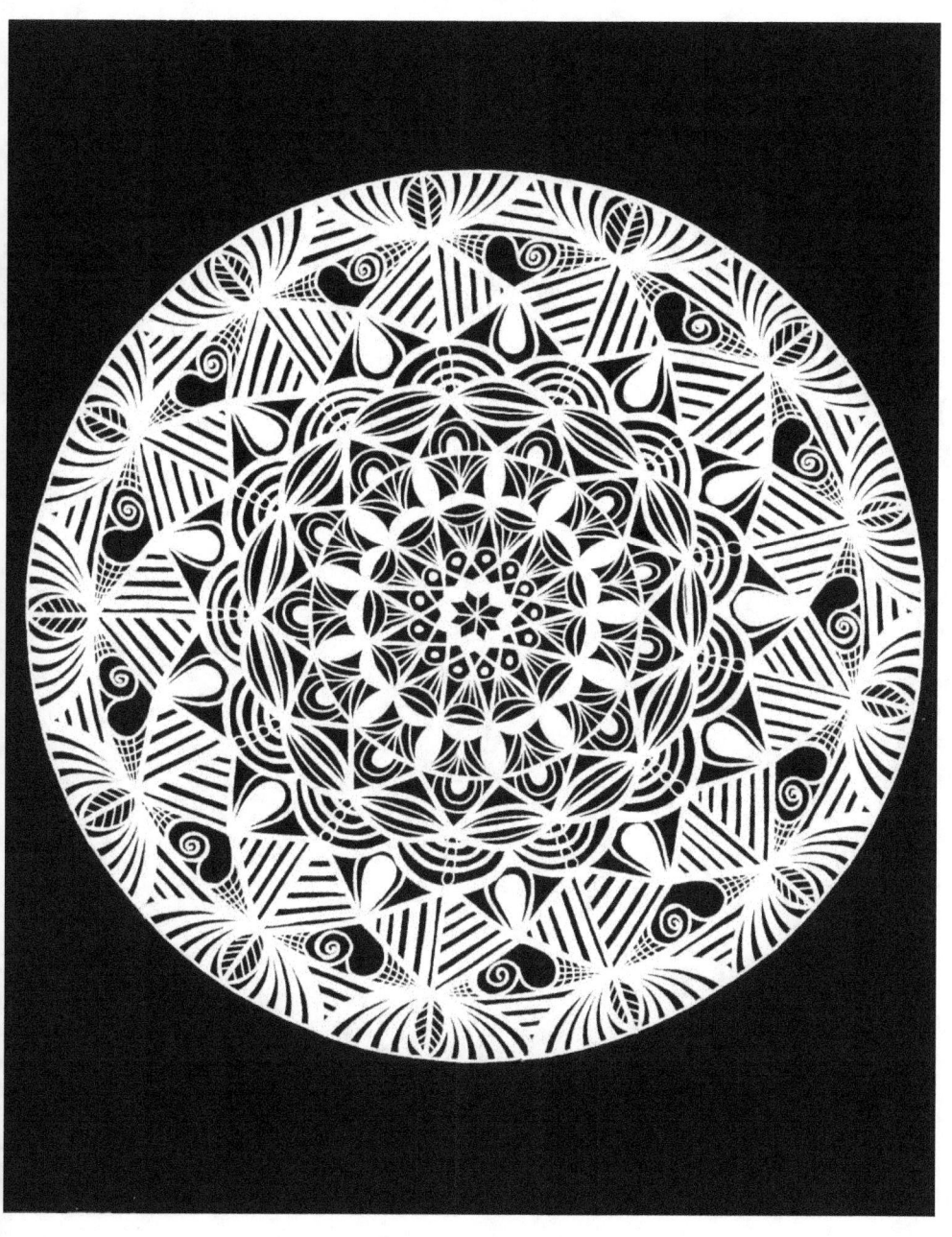

www.ingramcontent.com/pod-product-compliance
Lightning Source LLC
Chambersburg PA
CBHW070822180526
45168CB00002B/727